S. Childs Clarke

Festival and other hymns for church tides, and occasional services

S. Childs Clarke

Festival and other hymns for church tides, and occasional services

ISBN/EAN: 9783741183041

Manufactured in Europe, USA, Canada, Australia, Japa

Cover: Foto ©Angelika Wolter / pixelio.de

Manufactured and distributed by brebook publishing software
(www.brebook.com)

S. Childs Clarke

Festival and other hymns for church tides, and occasional services

FESTIVAL
AND OTHER HYMNS

FOR

CHURCH TIDES, AND OCCASIONAL SERVICES

TOGETHER WITH

LITANIES AND CAROLS

FOR VARIOUS SEASONS,

AND SONGS SACRED AND SECULAR.

BY

S. CHILDS CLARKE, M.A.,
VICAR OF THORVERTON, DEVON,

*Hon. Sec. of Exeter Diocesan Board of Education,
formerly Head Master of the Grammar School, Launceston.*

Author of "Thoughts in Verse, from a Village Churchman's Note Book";
"Harry Glenalmond"—a Cantata (with Music); "Memorial Tributes"
on Events in the Reign of Queen Victoria; "Services of Song for
Church Seasons"; "The Harvest Fields of Time" (Missionary Song
Service); "Children's Service and Festival Service"; "Musical
Setting of Marriage Service" (Music by Canon Hervey).

London:
SKEFFINGTON & SON, PICCADILLY, W.,
PUBLISHERS TO H.R.H. THE PRINCE OF WALES.
—
1896.

INSCRIBED,

BY PERMISSION,

AND WITH MUCH RESPECT,

TO

HIS GRACE, THE MOST REVEREND

FREDERICK TEMPLE,

LORD ARCHBISHOP OF CANTERBURY,

BY ONE,

WHO SERVED UNDER HIM

FOR MANY YEARS

IN HIS WESTERN DIOCESE.

PREFATORY NOTE.

The following Hymns, &c., have appeared from time to time in various Church Hymnaries, Periodicals, and in other collections.

The first eight Festival Hymns were contributed, by request, in successive years, to the London Gregorian Choral Festivals, and have been sung in S. Paul's and other Cathedrals.

It has always been esteemed by the Writer to be a very great privilege to be permitted to contribute to "The Service of Song in the House of the Lord," and he humbly trusts that some of the Hymns, now collected and published, may be of further use for this purpose.

Laus Deo.

Thorverton Vicarage, Devon,
    A.D. 1896.

. Application for permission to print any of these Hymns should be made to the Author.

CONTENTS.

Part I.—Sacred.

	PAGES
FESTIVAL AND OFFERTORY HYMNS	3—50
DEDICATION FESTIVAL HYMNS	51—55
MORNING AND EVENING	56—58
SUNDAY MORNING AND EVENING ...	59—62
FINAL SUNDAY EVENING	63—68

HYMNS FOR CHURCH SEASONS. *(From Song Services edited by the Author and A. H. Brown.)*

ADVENT-TIDE	69—72
CHRISTMAS-TIDE ...	73—76
PASSION-TIDE ...	77—90
EASTER-TIDE	91—93
ASCENSION-TIDE ...	94—97
WHITSUN-TIDE ...	98
FOR FLOWER SERVICES ...	99—105
HARVEST-TIDE	106—117

HYMNS FOR HOLY MATRIMONY	... 118—121
LITANIES FOR CHURCH SEASONS ...	... 122—135
OCCASIONAL HYMNS ...	... 136—159

	PAGES
FOR MISSIONARY SERVICES AND MEETINGS	160—164
HYMNS WRITTEN FOR PASSING EVENTS ...	165—169

CHILDREN'S HYMNS—

For Ordinary Services...	173—188
For Festival Services ...	189—201

CAROLS—

Christmas-tide ...	205—228
New Year	229
Easter-tide	230—248
Ascension-tide ...	249—252
Harvest-tide	253—261

Part II.—Secular.

ODES	265—271
SONGS ...	272—278
CHURCH DEFENCE SONGS ...	279—283
VOCAL TRIOS ...	284—287
PART SONGS ...	288—291
SONGS OF WELCOME AND GREETING	292—295
SCHOOL SONGS	296—298
TRANSLATIONS AND ADAPTATIONS FROM THE FRENCH	299—311

Acrostics.

INDEX OF FIRST LINES.

Part I.—Sacred.

	PAGE
All blessing, honour, glory, might	25
All hail, all hail to the Natal Day	76
All hail the time of gladness	224
Alleluia to Thee	103
Almighty Ruler of the world	23
As a beacon o'er the deep	161
As far as unto Bethany	251
As now before the mind	77
A Virgin did come	228
Awake, awake, with holy rapture sing	230
Awake my glory	231
Awhile the Victor vanquish'd lay	232
Because the sick and poor	104
Behold the MAN	83
Blessèd and Holy THREE	12
Blessèd LORD, Who for our learning	178
Brothers, ye must merry be	206
Brightly breaks the dawn of day	253
Carol we joyfully	249
CHRIST is risen from the dead	92
Church of the Living GOD	33
Come, for the night of gloom is o'er	233
Come, meek souls, whose lot is lowly	208
Come one and all	209
Come, Thou Blessed SPIRIT	186
Day of wonders, day of gladness	198
Dire and awful were the judgments	69

	PAGE
Each LORD'S Day has its eventide	66
Faithful in Thy love	107
Far up on high	185
FATHER, from Thy throne on high	131
FATHER, Who didst all things make	133
Firstlings of Martyrs	195
Forth to the waving seas of golden grain	254
FRAMER of the Light	56
From our childhood's early years ...	196
From out the dim and distant past	215
From out the spacious firmament	226
From the priceless Harvest ...	112
For these and countless mercies be	50
Gather, comrades, gather	139
Gather, Christian children	194
Gifts for mortals' gladness	101
Give ear unto our cry, O LORD	160
GOD is gone up	250
GOD of our strength, and our ROCK of salvation ...	27
Gracious GOD, another harvest...	110
Gracious FATHER, GOD of Love	134
Gracious LORD and MASTER	158
Gracious LORD of all Creation	99
Great Giver of all good	115
Hail, all hail this brightest morning	234
Hail, thou that art so highly grac'd ...	205
Hence all sorrow! Hence your fear ...	235
Holy Blessèd Trinity	130
Holy Blessèd Trinity *(Children's Service)*	187
Holy Trinity for ever Blessèd	199
Holy JESU, Heavenly KING	123
Holy JESU, when in grief	80
Hush'd is the din of battle ...	166
Hush! for around the fold	218
In a garden, once, when tempted	79

	PAGE
In all Thou didst while here on earth ...	184
In humble adoration	52
In life's long and weary warfare ...	46
In their MASTER'S Name ...	71
In the Name of GOD the FATHER	143
JESUS from above	197
JESU, Gracious LORD and MASTER	153
JESU, LORD and MASTER ...	155
JESU, LORD, ascended... ...	128
JESU, LORD, Thy Holy Presence	120
JESU, on this Blessed Morn ...	75
JESU, our opening year ...	122
JESU, Thou art aye the same ...	125
JESU, our LORD and GOD ...	29
Joyful is the Harvest-tide	200
Let Hosannas ring	196
Let Christians all rejoice to sing ...	210
Lift up your eyes and look upon the fields	163
Long since in by-gone days	145
Long look'd for Morn	211
Lo! Heaven's gates unfolding	95
Lo! plenteous is the Harvest	161
Lo! the Cross is rais'd on high ...	84
LORD, ere Thy day be o'er	65
LORD most Holy, GOD most mighty ...	142
LORD, once more Thy Day is done ...	64
LORD of power and might, the GIVER ...	150
LORD of the New Creation	39
LORD of all Creation	14
LORD, prevent us in our doings ...	67
LORD, we love the habitation	53
LORD, Who didst for us in Jordan ...	138
LORD, look down on us Thy servants ...	140
MAN He rose, since Man He died	236
'Mid gross darkness earth was lying	73
'Mid the loveliness of Spring-tide	237

	PAGE
None are so poor and none so weak	182
Not to seek our selfish pleasure	175
Now a New Year opens	181
Now amid the hills and vales	256
Now once more Thy Day is closing	176
Now once more we greet Thee	193
O Comforter of Zion's wastes	54
O come, lift up your eyes	255
O deep was the gloom	213
O dark and dreary Day	86
O Day of all days	240
Of newness is our song to-day	242
O GOD, most High, most Holy	87
O GOD, our Nation's Refuge	168
O GOD, Thou didst inspire	149
O HOLY GHOST, Who in primeval day	129
O Heavenly FATHER, GOD of Love	31
O kind and gentle SAVIOUR	190
O JESU, Who didst pass once more	127
O LAMB OF GOD, for sinners slain	162
O LORD, it is a joyful thing	57
O LORD, on this our festal day	10
Of old on slopes of Olivet	19
On, brothers, on	40
Once again, in glad reunion	152
Once again the Holy Season	212
Once more the sheaves are gather'd	115
On the Eve before the Sabbath	243
On our festal day	189
O SAVIOUR mine	81
O SPIRIT all pervading	98
O Thou, Who for man's sake	85
O Thou, Who dwellest in Eternity	51
O Thou, Who sojourning awhile	133
O Thou, Who didst the Eastern sages call	124
O Thou, the vast Creation's LORD	36
O Thou, by Whom all creatures live	50
Out of the deep	241

	PAGE
Pardon, Peace, Power *(Title)* ...	88
Pilgrims unto Zion	70
Put on thy strength, O Zion ...	109
Raise the strain of high thanksgiving ...	74
Raise we gladsome voices	147
Rejoice in your GOD, all ye people of earth	106
Remote, in distant days	94
Say, Who is this	78
See the guiltless Captive standing	82
The angel-music of the bells ...	177
Thee, GOD Almighty, we extol...	7
The stream of Life rolls on	180
The canopy of Heaven	105
The daughters of Jerusalem	238
The loving Shepherd smitten	245
The Psalmist's questions	96
The sheaf of First-fruits	91
The struggle with sin and death was o'er	248
Through dangers of the night	173
The weary world was hush'd in sleep ...	219
There is gladness in the air	246
There's a day that hearts of children ...	216
Thou, Who thro' shades of night ...	61
This world of ours was beautiful ...	220
Time's course ever onward	72
To Thee, our FATHER, GOD, and KING	21
To Thee, Who art the Harvest's LORD...	111
To our Heavenly FATHER	188
To CHRIST our Heavenly KING ...	191
To the presence chamber	118
To Thine House we come ...	100
To magnify Thy glorious Name	44
To purchase man's salvation ...	97
To Zion, stately Pile	3
Unto Thee, Most High	48
Unto flow'rets fair ...	102

	PAGE
Uplift your hearts	93
Up, for the glorious Autumn sun	257
Up the stately hill of Sion ...	42
Wake and sing the New Year's advent ...	229
Wake and with the early day	183
Wake once more a joyous strain ...	225
We strangers are and pilgrims	63
We bless our gracious GOD to-day ...	165
Welcome morn of joy and gladness ...	214
Welcome, welcome, Harvest-tide ...	260
We sing Thy coming, LORD, to-day ...	179
We sing a mighty wonder	222
When for all Thy saints departed ...	38
When sinks the Sun in western skies	174
When o'er lands in darkness shrouded	156
When the morning stars together	136
With thankful heart, with tuneful voice ...	114
With joyous festal strain	119
With joy we sing of Harvest	259
With Thee, O GOD, begun, with Thee shall close	16
With wary steps approach we	223

Part II.—Secular.

Adown the dells, on breezy hills	285
Ask not where is Beauty's dwelling	269
Come, schoolmates, let us jovial be	296
Come all, who bitter tears do shed	299
From old Dunheved's Castle wall	293
Hark! 'mid the stillness of the night ...	278
Home once more, to the dear old home	276
In palmy days of ancient Rome	297
If thou perceive thy soul to fill...	301

xv.

	PAGE
I hear along the street	307
It is the year of Jubilee	268
Little nurslings of the Winter	290
Lo! Autumn comes	303
Look forth! Look forth! a sail in sight	287
Loudly Dunheved's sons should sing ...	292
Oh, blithe and blest is Christmas-tide ...	275
O LORD of all Creation	291
Our grand old Church of England ...	279
Return, sweet Peace, for thee we sigh	273
Rouse ye, Devonia's sons, to-day	294
Ring out, ye bells, with blithesome peal ring out	267
Side by side, and hand in hand	274
Sing welcome to the Spring-time	284
Sleep, fairest lady	285
To arms, To arms, the trumpet call	282
The old village Church of our fathers	280
The sentinel his lone watch keeps	289
The war-trump echoes far and wide	288
Whence this Angel-host resplendent	309
With hopes so bright, in merriest mood	286
When shall the din of warfare cease	272
With fearless hearts and true, the Church's life-boats man	298
Yes, rise and come, mark how yon orb of day	265

Acrostics.

PART I.
Sacred.

FESTIVAL HYMNS.

*Processional Hymn.

"TO ZION, STATELY PILE."

Sung in S. Paul's Cathedral, by the United Choirs at the Festival, June 6th, a.d. 1889.

O Zion, stately Pile, †
   With joy her children come,
  Each sacred nave and aisle
   The wistful heart's true home!
          Sing Alleluia.

In solemn sequence sing,
  On this our festal day,
To Jesus, Salem's King,
  Awake and tune the lay.
          Sing Alleluia.

Yea, ready be each heart,
  Awake, O harp and lute!
Wake, bear your tuneful part,
  Nor strings nor voice be mute.
          Sing Alleluia.

---

* Written by request, and adapted to the ancient sequence—
    "Exultet laudibus
      Cœlestis curia."
Music harmonized by A. H. Brown.

† Zion means a heap of stones piled up, a monument set up.

PROCESSIONAL HYMN.

Ye people, clap your hands,
  And with melodious voice,
Ye white-rob'd minstrel bands
  In triumph-strain rejoice—
        Sing Alleluia.

The LORD ye glorify
  Is King o'er all the earth,
Laud ye His Majesty,
  O Choirs, in "rev'rent mirth,"
        Sing Alleluia.

He is gone up on high,
  In endless bliss to reign,
To Him all angels cry,
  We, with their countless train,
        Sing Alleluia.

* "The Holy Church below,
  Her expectation long,
Doth fairest union show
  With Heaven's choral song,"
        Sing Alleluia.

"Their life is not yet ours,
  But songs their hosts employ,
They, in celestial bowers,
  Amid their ceaseless joy"
        Sing Alleluia.

---

* "The Church triumphant and the Church below
In songs of praise their present union show;
Their joys are full, our expectation long;
In life we differ, but we join in song.
Angels and we, assisted by this art,
May sing together, tho' we dwell apart."
    Waller on Divine Poësie, circ. A.D. 1624.

"What tho' we dwell apart,
We strains together raise,
Fram'd in no earth-born art,
To swell our notes of praise,"
     Sing Alleluia.

The whole world is the LORD'S,
And they who therein dwell,
Life He to all affords,
And guards His Israël.
     Sing Alleluia.

The earth above the seas
He founded as of yore,
By His supreme decrees
He ruleth evermore.
     Sing Alleluia.

Ere long the LORD shall fill
With knowledge all the earth,
As by His Sovereign will
He gave the floods their birth.
     Sing Alleluia.

In ancient Israel's days *
They bore the ark along,
And 'mid their shouts of praise
They, in their festal song,
     Sang Alleluia.

To Zion's precincts press
GOD'S Israel to-day,
Their garb be Righteousness,
Of saints the meet array.
     Sing Alleluia.

---

* "Ascendit Deus, ascendit arca in Jerusalem cum cantu, Propheticè ascendit Christus in cœlum."—*Bossuet.*

Who shall the Holy Place
  Ascend? or who shall rise
To see unveiled that Face
  Where saints beyonds the skies
                Sing Alleluia.

How goodly and how fair
  Thine earthly temples, LORD!
Make glad each House of Prayer—
  Where all, in sweet accord,
                Sing Alleluia.

Set up Thyself, O GOD,
  Above the Heavenly height,
Thy glory spread abroad,
  While we, to praise Thy might,
                Sing Alleluia.

O risen LORD, with Thee
  May we in heart ascend;
In ages yet to be
  This strain shall know no end,
                Sweet Alleluia.

Thrice Holy, GOD, we raise
  Our festal songs to Thee,
Thine be co-equal praise,
  O Mystic Verity, Most Holy Trinity,
                Amen. Alleluia.

Festival Hymn.

SUNG IN S. PAUL'S CATHEDRAL AT THE FESTIVAL OF CHOIRS
(L.G.C.A.), A.D. 1890, AND IN EXETER CATHEDRAL, A.D. 1891.

THEE, GOD Almighty, we extol,
   As to Thy courts we press,
To join the strain of ceaseless praise
   Wherewith Thy creatures bless
"The Name, above all other names,"
   In filial love rever'd,
Mysterious, awe-inspiring Name!
   By guilty sinners feared.

Above the wingèd Cherubim
   Thou dwellest, O most High,
And yet in wondrous love dost deign
   These courts to sanctify,
By coming where Thy people meet,
   Of high and low degree—
All members of one brotherhood,
   Made brothers, LORD, by Thee.

Thine Israël here yield Thee thanks,
   As each his humble part
Amid the congregation takes
   From ground of loyal heart.
Our antiphons we raise in song,
   With rev'rent olden tones,
These, chanted by the Church of yore,
   Thy Church to-day still owns.

FESTIVAL HYMN.

Here, "how Thou goest," gracious God,
  In Thy majestic mien,
Amid these sacred precincts aye
  Thy footsteps may be seen;
The marshall'd singers go before,
  And next the minstrel train
In sweet accord their anthems raise,
  Thy praise—their glad refrain.

Thy God shall send forth strength for thee—
  His arm salvation brought:
That thing, we pray Thee, stablish still,
  That in us Thou hast wrought:
For Zion, for Thy temple's sake,
  So shall Thy people bring
With ready mind, with outstretch'd hand
  Each votive offering.

"City of our solemnities,"
  To thee our eyes we turn:
For thee, our quiet resting-place,
  Our hearts within us burn:
Thy tabernacles shall not fall;
  Thy cords men shall not break;
Nor from thy walls a single stone
  Shall rude destroyers take.

"For God is in the midst of thee,"
  Right early He shall give
To Zion help, to stablish her
  True life, in Him, to live.
"Go round about her palaces;
  Her bulwarks mark ye well,"
That so to all posterity
  Her refuge men may tell.

To Him we offer, as is meet,
  Best member that we have,
Since He—to bless His Sacred Name—
  To us that member gave;
Then open Thou our lips, O LORD,
  As we show forth Thy praise;
O fix our thoughts on Thee and Thine;
  Our earth-worn hearts upraise.

These festal days, like water-pools,
  Shine 'mid the world's drear waste;
How gracious in them, LORD, Thou art,
  Bid weary souls to taste.
"From off Thine altar touch these lips
  With coal of living fire":
With holy thoughts, with high resolve,
  Each glowing breast inspire.

"From strength to strength still go we on
  Till songs are ended here,
And each one in the courts above
  In Zion shall appear."
O Thou, "the One True Living GOD,
  The Everlasting King"—
Blest TRINITY, all praise be Thine,
  As in these courts we sing. Amen.

*Festival Hymn.

"O LORD, ON THIS OUR FESTAL DAY."

SUNG IN S. PAUL'S CATHEDRAL BY THE UNITED CHOIRS OF THE LONDON GREGORIAN CHORAL ASSOCIATION, A.D. 1891.

LORD, on this our Festal Day,
　　With marshall'd ranks, in long array
　　　Our solemn concourse wending,
Of thankfulness and joy our song—
Eastward our bourne these aisles along—
　　With voices duly blending.

We offer, FATHER, unto Thee
This tribute of our minstrelsy,
　　Thy Holy Name confessing:
And "with the multitude" we come
To this, "Thine House, of man the home,"
　　To seek Thy grace and blessing.

Faint semblance of those courts above—
This "Habitation," LORD, we love,
　　Wherein Thine honour dwelleth:
No earthly beauty may compare
With graces of Thy Temple fair,
　　Whose joy all joy excelleth.

Amid the longings that inflame
The saintly soul, one single aim
　　Each eager heart desireth—
With joy GOD's wondrous works to tell,
And in His Sanctuary dwell,
　　Where fondly man "enquireth." †

---

* Music by Arthur H. Brown.
† Psalm xxvii. 4.

Thy courts we enter, LORD, with praise,
To Thee our Antiphons we raise,
   The distant past proclaiming:
With tones, in days remote begun,
These handed on from sire to son,
   The Church's use still claiming.

Type of her constant unity,
We to her continuity
   Are ceaseless witness bearing:
Thus link we on the far off past
With years to come, while time shall last
   Her sacred truth declaring.

Thy waiting people everywhere
Adore Thy Name in praise and prayer,
   Thy mercies ever telling:
Here, laud and honour be to Thee,
O Holy, Blessed, Glorious Three,
   In this Thine earthly dwelling. Amen.

*Offertory Hymn.

SUNG IN S. PAUL'S CATHEDRAL, LONDON, AND IN EXETER CATHEDRAL AT THE FESTIVAL OF CHOIRS, A.D. 1892.

"Then the people rejoiced, for that they offered willingly, because with perfect heart they offered willingly to the Lord: and David the king also rejoiced with great joy."—1 CHRON. XXIX. 9.

BLESSÈD and Holy Three,
   SIRE and coequal SON,
  And gracious SPIRIT, unto Thee
   Be praise while ages run.
From Thee all good gifts come,
   Whereby Thy creatures live:—
Our health, our food, our joys of home
   Thou ceasest not to give.

LORD, we Thy servants taught
   That Thou wilt not disdain
Oblations to Thine Altar brought,
   Now offer them again:
Unworthy though we be,
   Through sins so manifold,
To bring in sacrifice to Thee
   The silver or the gold.

FATHER, accept, we pray,
   This bounden duty here,
And service we are met to pay,
   Who Thy great Name revere.
In this Thine house we plead
   The merits of Thy SON,
That He may pardon each misdeed
   And duty left undone.

---

* Music composed for this hymn by Sir John Stainer, Mus. Doc.

Ever Thy sick and poor
　Disciples true shall tend,
And, be it scant or full, their store
　On Thy glad service spend:
And precious in Thy sight
　Are tokens of their love—
The costly nard, the widow's mite,
　All treasur'd are above.

Merciful Saviour deign
　To sanctify each gift;
Thy waiting people ne'er in vain
　To Thee their hearts uplift.
In royal David's days
　The Hebrews joy'd to bring
To Thee their sacrifice of praise,*
　Their votive offering.

Ours be the mind that willed †
　Its choicest gifts to bring,—
"The perfect heart" with gladness filled
　Of Zion and her King.
So grant us here to-day,
　Before Thee to rejoice,
As we our homage come to pay,
　In gifts, in heart, in voice. Amen.

---

* " He that giveth alms sacrificeth praise."
† " If there be first a willing mind, it is accepted."

*Offertory Hymn.

SUNG AT THE FESTIVAL OF CHOIRS (L.G.C.A.), A.D. 1893,
IN S. PAUL'S CATHEDRAL, TO MUSIC COMPOSED
FOR IT BY G. C. MARTIN, MUS. DOC.

LORD of all creation,
    Now before Thy throne,
      We Thy people bring Thee
Gifts that are Thine own.
Thine is all the greatness,
    Power and glory Thine,
High o'er all exalted,
    Majesty Divine.
        Of Thine Own we offer,
          Of Thy gifts we give
        Unto Thee, O FATHER,
        In Whose life all live.

All the gold and silver,
    Corn on plains and hills,
Grass upon the mountains,
    Water in the rills—
All things yield Thee glory,
    With Thy Light they shine;
Thou all art inspirest—
    Science, skill, are Thine.
        Of Thine Own, &c.

---

* Written originally at the request of Reverend Canon Hervey, and sung at the re-opening of Sandringham Church, after restoration by H.R.H. the Prince of Wales. Sung, A.D. 1894, at Choral Festivals in the Cathedrals of Norwich and Truro, and at the Derby Archidiaconal Festival; also in Ely Cathedral, A.D., 1895. To be sung in Rochester Cathedral, A.D., 1897.

Body, Soul, and Spirit,
  Thought, and speech, and song,
Come of Thee, Creator,
  And to Thee belong,
These in bounden duty
  We devote to Thee;
Thine is all the dower,
  Thine the glory be.
      Of Thine Own, &c.

Of all works man doeth,
  None can greater be
Than the work devoted,
  O LORD GOD, to Thee:
Hither all to serve Thee,
  Rich and poor repair,
Joy awaits Thy people
  In Thy House of Prayer.
      Of Thine Own, &c.

Alms-deeds, prayers, and praises,
  With "the willing mind,"
In the Name of JESUS,
  Shall acceptance find.
Evermore thanksgiving
  To the FATHER, SON,
And the gracious SPIRIT,
  Blessèd Three in One.
      Still Thy Church shall offer,
        Of Thy gifts shall give
      Unto Thee, the Giver,
        In Whose life all live. Amen.

*Festival Hymn.

SUNG IN S. PAUL'S CATHEDRAL, JUNE 7TH, A.D. 1894, BY THE UNITED CHOIRS OF THE LONDON GREGORIAN CHORAL ASSOCIATION.

"The Lord is my Light and my Salvation . . . The Lord is the Strength of my life . . . ."

WITH Thee, O GOD, begun, with Thee shall close
　　Our Evensong.
　Strength of our life, each day
　Thou art our Staff and Stay;
　'Mid darkness of the night
　Thou art our soul's true Light—
With Thee, O GOD, begun, with Thee shall close
　　Our Evensong.

One thing do we desire, one thing require
　　Of Thee, O LORD,
　That we, Thine Israel,
　Within Thine House may dwell,
　There all our days to be,
　And Thy fair beauty see—
This one thing we desire, and this require
　　Of Thee, O LORD.

For us, in time of trouble, Thou shalt hide
　　Within Thy gates:
　Yea, in Thy secret place
　Our refuge shall we trace,
　For Thou wilt set Thine own
　Upon a rock of stone,
And us in time of trouble Thou wilt hide
　　Within Thy gates.

---

* Music by Arthur H. Brown.

Oblations, therefore, FATHER, we will bring
        With gladness great,
        Uplifted hands shall be
        Our Sacrifice to Thee,
        As we our voices raise
        In heartfelt songs of praise
When we oblations to the FATHER bring
        With gladness great.

Whene'er, as incense, we set forth our prayer,
        In mercy hear,
        For Thou of yore hast said
        As men Thy courts did tread,
        "SEEK YE MY FACE,"—Lo, now
        Before Thy Face we bow:
And when, as incense, we set forth our prayer,
        In mercy hear.

Hide not Thyself, ere for the world again,
        These courts we leave:
        Thy succour, Gracious LORD,
        Thou ever dost afford:
        Thy servants ne'er forsake,
        Them 'neath Thy wing O take,
Nor hide Thy face, ere for the world again,
        These courts we leave.

Thy people utterly should faint and fail,
        Bereft of Thee;
        Thy goodness, we believe,
        We shall through life receive,
        Frail children of the dust
        In Thee alone we trust,
For utterly Thy people faint and fail,
        Bereft of Thee.

FESTIVAL HYMN.

For graces, gifts, and mercies Thee we bless,
O TRIUNE GOD,
Hosanna unto Thee,
O GOD the FATHER, be—
Hosanna to the WORD,
And HOLY GHOST adored;
In ceaseless Alleluias Thee we bless,
O TRIUNE GOD. Amen.

*Processional Hymn.

F old, on slopes of Olivet
Their LORD and King the Hebrews met,
With scattered boughs and waving palms,
The burden of their festal Psalms—
  Hosanna, LORD,
  Hosanna in the Highest!

To JESUS, as He rides along,
The multitudes their triumph song
Upraise, to welcome Sion's King,
While far and near the echoes ring—
  Hosanna, LORD,
  O save us, we beseech Thee.

And thus by David's Royal Son
The mighty conquest was begun,
Erelong on blood-stained Calvary
Its full accomplishment to see.
  Hosanna, LORD,
  Hosanna in the Highest!

For ever "blessèd He Who came
In GOD the LORD JEHOVAH'S Name."
That He for all might Ransom be
To "send them true prosperity."
  Hosanna, LORD,
  Hosanna in the Highest!

---

* Sung at L.G.C.A. Festival, in S. Paul's, A.D. 1895, to music by A. H. Brown; also at the Truro Choral Festival, in the Cathedral, A.D. 1896, music by T. Roylands-Smith.

And while to-day with gladsome feet
Thy Courts we tread, our King to greet,
That olden Paschal Hymn's refrain
We joy to echo once again—
    Hosanna, LORD,
    Hosanna in the Highest!

To us Thy SPIRIT, LORD, impart—
Grant us the "meek and lowly heart,"
Vouchsafe us all humility
That we may Thy disciples be—
    Hosanna, LORD,
    Hosanna in the Highest!

So shall our praises reach Thy Throne,
So wilt Thou take us for Thine Own,
When we Thy ransomed people meet
And bow before Thy Mercy-seat.
    Hosanna, LORD,
    Hosanna in the Highest!

And when all earthly strife is done,
When we, through Thee, have victory won,
May we, with Angel Host on high,
And with Thy Church triumphant cry—
    Alleluia,
    All glory in the Highest!
      Amen.

*Offertory Hymn.

"I will give Thee thanks in the great congregation, I will praise Thee among much people."—PSALM XXXV. 18.

TO Thee, our FATHER, GOD, and King,
    Thy humble servants come to bring
      Their sacrifice of praise:
"Among much people," LORD, will we
Our meet thanksgiving unto Thee
      With hearts and voices raise.

O Fount of Life, in Whom all live,
Who Thy good gifts to all dost give,
      How shall we meet Thy claim?
Unworthy ever, at our best
To serve our King at His behest,
      And glorify His Name.

Yet whoso praise doth offer here,
And in these sacred courts appear,
      Shall Thine acceptance find;
Thou wilt not humblest gifts disdain,
No off'rings wilt Thou reckon vain
      From glad and willing mind.

Thy bounty doth the whole world fill,
As in the days of old, so still
      All must the Giver own,
And unto Him Who all things gave
Their presents bring of what they have,
      To lay before His Throne.

---

* Written by request of the Committee of the L.G.C.A., to tune 139 Hymns A. and M., and sung at their Festival in S. Paul's Cathedral, A.D. 1896.

OFFERTORY HYMN.

No gain to Thee, LORD, can accrue
From gifts of ours;—of works we do
   We know Thou hast no need,
Yet Thou dost graciously command
That we, the creatures of Thine hand,
   Shall render Thee due meed.

Our joy be ever to draw near
Thy mercy-seat in faith and fear
   Until this Life be o'er:
Then Faith and Hope shall merge in Love,
Where in the blissful realms above
   Thou reignest evermore.

Eternal FATHER, Thee we bless,
Thy co-eternal SON confess
   And SPIRIT, Three in One:
Thee we adore, in Thee believe,
Who praise and glory shalt receive
   While endless ages run. Amen.

Processional Hymn.

"LAUS ET GLORIA IN EXCELSIS."

ALMIGHTY Ruler of the world to Thee,
Abiding ever in eternity,
From us and all Thy Church ascribèd be
    Praise and glory in the highest.

All laud and honour unto Thee belong,
Of Thee we sing these earthly courts among,
Thine be the tribute of our festal song—
    Praise and glory in the highest.

The multitude of Isles that on Thee wait,
Do raise in lofty or in lowly state
Their meed of song within Thy temple gate—
    Praise and glory in the highest.

And they who rest in Paradise, unite
Their strains with ours, amid those realms of light,
To tell of all Thy mercy and Thy might—
    Praise and glory in the highest.

And all the Heavenly Host beyond the sky,
Angel and Seraph with Archangel vie
Thine hallow'd Name, O LORD, to glorify—
    Praise and glory in the highest.

---

* Sung in Exeter Cathedral, A.D. 1893, Bristol Cathedral, A.D. 1894, Priory Church, Cartmel, Archdeaconry of Furness, A.D. 1894, at the Festival of Choirs; at the opening of the organ, Paignton, Devon, A.D. 1896. Music by Sir Joseph Barnby.

Whene'er we tread Thy Courts, may all around
Serve to uplift our souls, while sight and sound
Bid us reflect we stand on holy ground—
    Praise and glory in the highest.

Of old Thou didst in glowing light appear,
When foemen to Thine Israel drew near,
Inspiring these with faith and those with fear—
    Praise and glory in the highest.

So shield Thy servants from temptation now,
And with Thy "Fire or love" our souls endow,
As we before Thy Mercy-seat do bow—
    Praise and glory in the highest.

Illumine with Thy blessèd SPIRIT's rays
Our hearts, and tune our lips to swell Thy praise,
So shall we render on these holy days
    Praise and glory in the highest.

And when all festal strains of earth are o'er,
To Thee, O TRIUNE GOD, may we outpour
With all Thy Church triumphant evermore
    Praise and glory in the highest.
          Amen.

*Hymn of Praise to "The Lamb Slain."

Founded on the Revelation of S. John, Chapters v. and vii.

SUNG IN NORWICH CATHEDRAL, A.D. 1894, AT DERBY ARCHI-
DIACONAL FESTIVAL, A.D. 1894, AT THE FESTIVAL OF CHOIRS.

ALL blessing, honour, glory, might,
    In Heaven and earth and sea
      Ten thousand times ten thousand sing,
As they their ceaseless offering
Of praise, O LORD, do yield to Thee.

From ev'ry kindred, tribe, and tongue,
    Shall rise before Thy Throne
The sweet refrain of that "New Song,"
To laud the LAMB Thy Courts among,
From all who Thy Salvation own.

For Thou wast slain, and hast redeemed
    Our sinful souls from death—
Thy wondrous mercy hast display'd,
Thy people kings and priests hast made,
Who erst didst give them life and breath.

And "Thou all riches, wisdom, strength,
    Art worthy to receive";
All glory, honour, power, are Thine,
Adored in Majesty Divine,
In Thee we trust, in Thee believe.

---

* Music by Mendelssohn. Arranged for this Hymn by Sir J. Stainer, Mus. Doc.

HYMN OF PRAISE TO "THE LAMB SLAIN."

In white robes clad, and in their hands
   The palms of victory,
The ransom'd souls and angel choir,
With voices loud that never tire,
Pour forth their songs eternally.

With Angels and Archangels, now
   Henceforth and evermore,
We laud and magnify Thy Name,
Whose glory Heaven and earth proclaim,
Whom all Creation doth adore. Amen.

Peculiar metre (five lines) written for the Music by request.

*Hymn for a Choral Festival.

TO BE SUNG AT THE NORWICH FESTIVAL, A.D. 1897,
TO MUSIC BY DR. J. F. BRIDGE.

"Be Thou my strong Habitation, whereunto I may continually resort: Thou hast given commandment to save me; for Thou art my Rock and my Fortress."—PSALM LXXI. 3.

GOD of our Strength and our Rock of Salvation,
    Stay of our souls amid life's stormy sea,
Worthy art Thou to receive adoration,
    Hearts with our voices uplifting to Thee.

Here would we offer Thee, FATHER forgiving,
    Fruit of our lips on this festival day,
Sojourning yet in the land of the living,
    Wending, as pilgrims, on life's weary way.

Thee and Thy faithfulness, LORD of Creation,
    With the bright Seraphim join we to praise,
Hymning Thy glory in deep veneration,
    While in these outer courts anthems we raise.

Meed of our minstrelsy to Thine House bringing,
    Our bounden duty shall be our delight;
"Fain shall our lips be" the while we are singing
    Here of Thy righteousness, mercy and might.

Thou art the changeless One ever abiding
    'Mid all the changes and chances of life,
Under Thy wing all Thy chosen ones hiding,
    Safe in Thy keeping from earth's daily strife.

---

* Written to music by Rev. A. W. Hamilton-Gell.

HYMN FOR A CHORAL FESTIVAL.

Thou through the deep gloom our pathway canst brighten,
    Thou in all sorrows our spirit canst cheer,
Thou all our manifold burdens dost lighten,
    Guiding our feet in our pilgrimage here.

Feeble and faint all our songs of devotion,
    Earth-worn our hearts—yet shall hope's kindly ray
Kindle within us each holy emotion,
    As in Thy temple our homage we pay.

Be now and ever our "Strong Habitation,"
    From sin's dominion O grant us release,
Thou art, LORD JESU, our soul's aspiration,
    From Thee is pardon and in Thee is peace.

FATHER, on Thee Thy frail children depending,
    We faint and fail when we wander alone,
Grant us sweet foretaste of bliss never ending,
    Shared by the ransomed encircling Thy Throne. Amen.

N.B.—Verse 2 can be omitted if the hymn be required for general use.

Festival Hymn.

SET TO MUSIC BY DR. G. C. MARTIN, ORGANIST OF S. PAUL'S
CATHEDRAL, AND SUNG AT THE FESTIVAL OF
CHURCH CHOIRS, A.D. 1895.

"On His Head were many crowns."

ESU, our LORD and GOD,
    Worthy art Thou
  Of all the glorious crowns
    Circling Thy brow:
Thy Church throughout the world
    On Thee doth call,
Ever confessing Thee
    Our "ALL in all."

By Thee the worlds were framed
    In times of yore:
Glad tidings from Thee spread
    All the world o'er:
Of their deliverance
    Captives have heard,
Loud sounds the Gospel Trump,
    Thou art "The WORD."

Weary worn wayfarers
    Journeying on,
'Till this life's pilgrimage
    Be past and gone:
Guidance they seek from Thee,
    Tempted to stray
In Satan's devious paths;
    Thou art "The WAY."

FESTIVAL HYMN.

Saviour, to Thee we turn
  When doubts arise,
Springing from mists of earth,
  Blinding our eyes.
Thou canst enlighten us,
  In age and youth,
Bidding the darkness flee ;
  Thou art "The Truth."

Giver of all good gifts,
  All fulness dwells
In Thee—of wants supplied
  Thy goodness tells :
Wounded we cry to Thee,
  In deadly strife
Thou art sin's Conqueror,
  Thou art "The Life."

Star of the East, arise,
  Bright is Thy ray,
Day-spring and Harbinger
  Of endless day.
Perfect the work in us
  Thou hast begun,
Jesu, of Righteousness
  Thou art " The Sun."

" Buckler and Shield Thou art,
  O Triune Lord,
" Refuge and Strong Defence "
  Thou dost afford :
Hear now, and evermore,
  Thy people's call,
Be through eternity
  Our "All in all." Amen.

*Festival Hymn.

TO THE HOLY TRINITY.

"O praise God in His holiness."
"There is mercy with Thee, therefore shalt Thou be feared."

HEAVENLY FATHER, GOD of love,
With Thee is mercy, therefore Thee we fear:
Thy pardon we would crave when we draw near,
    To bow before Thy throne,
    Our sinfulness to own,
        O GOD of love.

O KING of kings, O LORD of lords,
Who grantest us to live, to move, to be,—
This life be ours to consecrate to Thee;
    Accept the prayer and praise
    Which in Thine House we raise,
        O LORD our GOD.

O Son of Man, O GOD with us,
With man in all his weakness Thou dost feel,
E'en still, as MAN, to men Thyself reveal:
    Thine was the lowly birth
    To raise the sons of earth,
        O WORD made Flesh.

O CHRIST, O LORD our Righteousness,
Our humble off'ring Thou wilt not disdain,
As here with falt'ring lips we sing again
    Our anthems, when we meet
    Before Thy Mercy-seat,
        O Great High PRIEST.

---

* Written to music by Arthur H. Brown.

FESTIVAL HYMN.

O Heavenly Dove, O Paraclete,
Who dost enkindle with celestial fire
These souls of ours, and holy love inspire,—
    Thou makest hearts to burn,
    As unto God they turn,
        O Fire of love.

"Thrice Holy Fount, Thrice Holy Fire,"
Instil into our hearts the love of Thee:
Then worthier shall our feeble offering be,
    When to our own true Home,
    Our Father's House, we come,
        O Fount of life.

O Trinity, O Unity,
One God, in Persons Three, Thy name we bless,
And praise Thee in Thine awful holiness;
    Be with us on our way
    Throughout Life's little day,
        Jehovah, God.

*Festival Hymn.

SET TO MUSIC BY BERTHOLD TOURS.

"Blessed be the Lord God of Israel from everlasting, and world without end."—PSALM CVI. 48.

"He hath put a New Song in my mouth."—PSALM XL. 3.

CHURCH of the Living GOD,
    Take up thy song,
  To glorify JEHOVAH'S Name
    His Courts among:
      In gladsome praise
      Thy notes upraise—
CHRIST with His Church now deigns to dwell,
    His Kingdom Thou!—O Israel.

    The vast unbroken chain
      Of living souls
  Shall laud and magnify Thee, LORD,
      While onward rolls
      Song's ceaseless tide
      From far and wide—
For with His Church CHRIST deigns to dwell,
    His Kingdom Thou!—O Israel.

    From highest Angel Host
      Around Thy Throne,
  To humblest denizens of earth,
      Thy might they own;
      Their LORD they bless,
      Thy Name confess,
Since with His Church CHRIST deigns to dwell,
    His Kingdom Thou!—O Israel.

---

* Set to music by A. H. Brown, for the L.G.C.A. Festival, A.D. 1897.

O Zion, wake and sing—
　　Take for thy strain
The Lord's "New Song," and echo on
　　Its sweet refrain—
　　Meet offering
　　Be thine to bring,
For with His Church Christ deigns to dwell,
　　His Kingdom Thou!—O Israel.

In Him Thou art renew'd—
　　By His dread strife!
His own New Covenant proclaims
　　Newness of Life;
　　His mercies sure
　　For aye endure,
And with His Church He deigns to dwell,
　　His Kingdom Thou!—O Israel.

Age after age proclaims
　　The wondrous theme
First caroll'd by the Heavenly Host;
　　When to redeem
　　The sons of earth
　　And give new birth
He came, thenceforward here to dwell,
　　His Kingdom Thou!—O Israel.

Praise to the Tri-une God
　　Whom we adore;
No "strangers now, nor foreigners"—
　　For evermore
　　His heirs to be,
　　Joint heirs are we
With Christ the Lord, Emmanuel,
　　His Kingdom Thou!—O Israel.

In Heaven "Trisagion"
    They ever sing:
Shall man, redeemed and sanctified,
    No tribute bring?
    O TRINITY,
    O UNITY,
The One True GOD—grant us to dwell
    With Thee, and be Thine Israel. Amen.

Festival Hymn.

"To the end that my glory may sing praise unto Thee and not be silent."—PSALM XXX. 12 (Bible Version).

 THOU, the vast Creation's LORD, Most High,
    Who in the Heav'n of Heavens hast Thy dwelling,
We humbly to Thy mercy-seat draw nigh,
    Thine endless Love Thy boundless might forth telling.

Celestial Hosts of Angels came of Thee,
    The wingèd Cherubim were Thy creation:
In ceaseless song they laud Thy Majesty,
    *Taught by Thy Church the wonders of Salvation.

Man lower than the Angels Thou didst make,
    His wondrous frame Thy handy-work proclaiming:
Him for Thy child, Thine erring child, dost take,
    As Thine,—his body, soul and spirit claiming.

O FATHER uncreate, the day is Thine,
    Thou in the shades of night the earth enfoldest:
By Thee first kindled Heaven's lights do shine,
    The mighty Ocean in Thine hand Thou holdest.

The glorious Sun his daily course to run,
    E'en as a giant, in his might, rejoices:
From early dawn until each day is done,
    Thy praise is chanted in "earth's many voices."

---

*Eph. iii. 10.

Still year by year Thou stretchest forth Thine hand,
  With plenteousness Thou fillest all things living;
The clouds drop gentle rain at Thy command,
  To hills and vales and plains fresh verdure giving.

LORD, what is man that Thou should'st mindful be
  Of him? yet Thou art ever gifts bestowing:
While grace from Thine exhaustless treasury
  In copious showers, to bless Thy Church, is flowing.

Onward we journey to the promised Land,
  The saving strength of Thy right hand is o'er us:
Faith, Hope, and Love inspire our pilgrim band,
  Thy Holy Presence goeth on before us.

Awake, then, "glory," lute and harp awake,
  To laud Thy Name love shall our hearts awaken:
As through these sacred courts our way we take,
  By worldly ills "cast down but not forsaken."

Our heaviness Thou turnest into joy,
  In place of sackcloth girding us with gladness:
To bless Thy Name shall be our tongue's employ,
  Its "glory" thus to be amid Life's sadness.

Our hearts are fixed, our hearts are fixed, to Thee,
  O, TRI-UNE LORD, our grateful praise we tender:
Our Evensong, as incense, here shall be,
  *"Calves of our lips"—the sacrifice we render.
                        Alleluia. Amen.

---

* Hosea xiv. 2.

*Processional Hymn for S. Clement's Day.

"Which Hope we have as an Anchor of the Soul, both sure and steadfast, and which entereth into that within the veil."
—HEBREWS VI. 19.

"Be ye followers of me, even as I also am of Christ."
—1 COR. XI. 1.

WHEN for all Thy Saints departed,
   JESU, LORD, Thy Name we bless,
And for Martyrs noble-hearted,
   Who, in life-long holiness,
Sought and found Thy great Salvation;
   'Mid the foremost of that band,
Gathered out of every Nation,
   We behold Saint Clement stand.

His the Anchor—well-earned TOKEN—
   "Entering in within the veil;"
When the golden bowl was broken,
   Hope did then Thy Saint avail.
Sweet the message from his pages,
   As of gentle Peace they tell,
Echoing on throughout the ages
   To the Church he lov'd so well.

When Thy people come before Thee,
   Gracious LORD, these Courts among,
When, to worship and adore Thee,
   We upraise our Festal Song,
May no listless supplication
   Rise from hearts, or dull or cold;
Earnest be our dedication,
   Following Thy Saint of old.

---

* Written by request, and set to music by F. W. Goodrich, Organist of S. Clement's, Notting Hill.

PROCESSIONAL HYMN FOR S. CLEMENT'S DAY.

Prelate, Prophet, Priest and Martyr
 In Thy Servant, LORD, we see,
Who for all the world would barter
 His reward and rest with Thee?
As through life we journey onward,
 Brightly may his banner shine,
Leading on and pointing upward,
 Till we be for ever Thine.

JESU, King of Saints, we bless Thee
 For Thy pattern earthly life;
Prince of Martyrs, we confess Thee,
 Victor in the last dread strife.
Thee, in Thy eternal Union
 With the FATHER, we adore,
With the HOLY GHOST communion,
 LORD, vouchsafe us evermore. Amen.

*Festival Hymn.

"ON, BROTHERS, ON TO THE BETTER LAND."

SUNG AT THE EXETER FESTIVAL OF CHOIRS, A.D. 1895.

> "Yet Thou in Thy manifold mercies forsookest them not in the wilderness; the pillar of the cloud departed not from them by day to lead them in the way; neither the pillar of fire by night, to shew them light, and the way wherein they should go."
> —NEHEMIAH IX. 19.

ON, brothers, on to the better land,
    Chanting our songs in triumphal strain,
    Shoulder to shoulder marches our band—
    On, till the golden gates we gain!
Forward our steps to the Home beyond,
    Seeking the country yet unseen,
Where to our hopes shall at last respond
    Glories untold in dazzling sheen.
    On, brothers, on to the better land,
        Chanting our songs in triumphal strain,
    On, ever onward the march of our band,
        "Onward," our pilgrim song's refrain!

Led by the pillar of cloud by day,
    Israel journeyed amid the wild;
Nightly, the fiery pillar's ray
    March of that lonesome host beguiled:

---

* Set to music by D. J. Wood, Mus. Doc., organist of Exeter Cathedral. Set to music also by W. J. Spinney, and sung at the Festival of Choirs at Leamington. And by F. W. Goodrich, and sung in the Crystal Palace by 6,000 voices at a Festival.

FESTIVAL HYMN.

God for their Guardian, God their Guide,
  God 'gainst the foe for His people fought.
God at the Jewish warriors' side—
  They to their promised land were brought.
      On, brothers, on to the better land, &c.

Onward the march of the Christian host,
  On through the world's dread wilderness;
Christ for our Captain, His Name we boast,
  Jesus the Lord our Righteousness;
Under His banner sworn to fight,
  Journey we onward day by day;
Comrades, we trust in the Victor's might,
  We shall be victors in the fray.
      On, brothers, on to the better land, &c.

Perils may come, and the storm-clouds rise,
  Foemen may threaten, snares abound;
God sets His rainbow in darksome skies,
  Angels our path shall compass round.
On, let us on, till the march be done,
  Strong in the Leader's strength we stand;
Forward we press till the prize be won—
  Rest, endless Peace—the Fatherland.
      On, brothers, on to the better land, &c.
                      Amen.

*Festival Hymn.

"They have seen Thy goings, O God, even the goings of my God, my King, in the Sanctuary. The singers went before, the players on the instruments followed after."

UP the stately hill of Sion
   In the olden Hebrew days,
  At their Holy Convocations
   Onward to the strains of praise,
Singing songs they lov'd so well
Marched the tribes of Israel.

"In Thy goings" then they saw Thee,
  Mighty GOD, Eternal King,
When Thy Sanctuary treading,
  All its Courts they caused to ring
With their notes of festal song
As Thine Ark they bore along.

Foremost came the band of singers
  Marching with a measur'd tread,
Skilful minstrels follow after,
  Who the swelling chorus led,
While with trumpets' thrilling sound
Harps and psalteries resound.

Unto Sion's sacred precincts
  Still Thy faithful people press,
There Thy meed of praise to offer
  In fair garb of holiness;
Thee, our GOD and King we claim
As we laud Thy Holy Name.

---

* Set to music by Dr. Geo. C. Martin, organist of S. Paul's Cathedral, and sung at the Festival of the London Church Choir Association, in S. Paul's, November 28th, 1895.

FESTIVAL HYMN.

Rang'd in ranks of goodly order
  On this joyous festal day,
Whither Thou, High Priest, dost lead us,
  We, Thy minstrels wend our way.
"How Thou goest" still is seen,
Thou art still as Thou hast been.

Heavenly FATHER, we Thy children
  At Thy bidding come to Thee,
In Thine Holy House to offer
  Prayer and praise adoringly,
Here before Thee to rejoice
In Thy Courts with gladsome voice.

JESU, when with Alleluias,
  Thee Thy waiting people greet,
When within Thine House assembled
  We draw nigh Thy mercy-seat,
Thou didst promise still to be
With Thy people ceaselessly.

Gracious SPIRIT, Thou inspirest
  Earth-worn hearts with Heavenly love,
"Our infirmities" Thou helpest,
  Thine—the unction from above.
Thine—our souls in prayer to raise,
Thine "intoning voice"—our praise.

Unto Thee, TRIUNE JEHOVAH,
  FATHER, SON, and HOLY GHOST,
Sing we Holy, Holy, Holy.
  Church on earth and Heavenly Host
Alleluias now outpour,
Alleluia, evermore. Amen.

Processional Hymn.

"His Name shall endure for ever: His Name shall be continued as long as the sun: and men shall be blessed in Him: all nations shall call Him blessed. Blessed be the Lord God, the God of Israel, Who only doeth wondrous things. And blessed be His glorious Name for ever: and let the whole earth be filled with His glory; Amen, and Amen."—PSALM LXXII. 17, 18, 19.

TO magnify Thy glorious Name,
O LORD, we now draw near,
Encouraged by Thy gracious Word
Before Thee we appear:
And as we tread Thy sacred courts
Our Antiphon be here—
"For ever shall Thy Name endure."

For when that Name rever'd we sing,
When Thee we praise and bless:
Thy loving-kindness fills our souls,—
Constrains us to confess
All Thou hast done, and doest still—
"The LORD our Righteousness,"—
"For ever shall Thy Name endure."

From sire to son, in ages past,
That Name was handed on,
And in the ages yet to come
Its kindly light shall dawn,
And still shall shine with changeless ray
When time itself is gone—
"For ever shall Thy Name endure."

PROCESSIONAL HYMN.

With glad accord our hearts we raise:—
* "To Thy most Holy Name,
And to remembrance, LORD, of Thee
Our soul's desire"!—we claim
Our sonship in Thy family
And sing with glad acclaim
"For ever shall Thy Name endure."

While from the East, to Western skies
O'er earth shines forth the sun,
Rejoicing as a giant still
His daily course to run,
So shall Thy blessèd Name remain,
Thy holy will be done,
Yea, "ever shall that Name endure."

JESU, LORD GOD of Israel,
Who hast done wondrous things,
Who from earth's darkness didst arise
With healing on Thy wings,
Each nation under Heav'n to Thee
Its benediction brings—
"For ever shall Thy Name endure."

The Church Thy Majesty Divine
Shall never cease to praise;
With Angels and the Heavenly Host
Shall strains of blessing raise:
Amen, and yet Amen be ours
Throughout the endless days.
"For ever blessèd be Thy Name."

---

* Isaiah xxvi. 8.

*Festival Hymn.

" Them will I bring to My Holy Mountain, and make them joyful in My House of Prayer . . . for Mine House shall be called an House of Prayer for all nations."—ISAIAH LVI. 7.

  IN life's long and weary warfare,
   Oft in gloom, and darksome mood,
  We may hear a voice that whispers
   " Who will shew us any good ? "
  Then unto Thy Courts, O FATHER,
   We, Thy children, would repair,
  Thou wilt make Thy servants joyful,
   They shall find the answer there.

  When borne down by weight of sorrow
   Or by load of care opprest—
  Whither shall we turn for solace?
   Whither flee to find our rest?
  Thither, where, in joyous spring-tide,
   For their "house" the sparrows hie,
  When their tender brood they cherish
   Round Thine altars, O Most High.

  If vexations sorely try us
   'Mid our deep distress of mind,
  When perplexing doubts distract us,
   Can we then no refuge find?—
  In Thine "amiable dwellings,"
   LORD OF HOSTS, our GOD and KING,
  Where " a nest the swallow findeth,"
   Weary wanderer welcoming.

---

* Written to music by Dr. Geo. C. Martin, organist of S. Paul's Cathedral.

FESTIVAL HYMN.

When the hands hang down beside us,
  When no help our weakness sees,
What shall brace the limbs that languish?
  What make strong the feeble knees?
To Thy Sanctuary turn we,
  There to lift the drooping hands,
"Out of Zion Thou shalt strengthen"
  All Thy frail and fainting bands.

We are pilgrims, and we journey
  "Thro' the vale of misery";
Thro' the wild so waste and barren—
  Can we no refreshment see?
Yea—for "as a well we use it"
  'Mid the dry and parchèd ground;
Here the springs of living water
  By GOD's faithful ones are found.

Tho' our strains be faint and feeble,
  These Thine outer courts among,
This shall be our "Sursum Corda," *
  This our cheery pilgrim song—
Glory be to GOD the FATHER,
  Glory be to GOD the SON,
Glory be to GOD the SPIRIT;
  One in Three and Three in One.
                Alleluia! Amen.

---

* i.e., "*Lift up your hearts.*" In use in the English Church for many centuries.

*Festival Hymn.

WRITTEN TO MUSIC BY REV. J. B. DYKES, MUS. DOC.

"*We assemble and meet together—
To render thanks for the great benefits received at His hands,
To set forth His most worthy praise,
To hear His Most Holy Word, and
To ask those things which are requisite and necessary as well
for the body as the soul.*"—PRAYER BOOK EXHORTATION.

UNTO Thee, Most High,
   Humbly we draw nigh,
     Who loyal liegemen of our LORD would be,
   Service pure and true
   Is from all hearts due
Who worship Thine Eternal Majesty.

   Here "will we" to-day
   " With the spirit pray, †
And with the understanding " lift our voice :
   And to Thee, O KING,
   " With the spirit sing,"
While with the understanding we rejoice.

   From Thy Church we learn,
   When aside we turn
From worldly ways and thoughts to seek Thy face,
   How, 'mid Life's unrest,
   We may serve Thee best
When in these Courts we glorify Thy Name.

---

* Printed in the Service Book of the London Association of Church Choirs for their Festival in S. Paul's Cathedral, November, A.D. 1896.

† 1 Cor. xiv. 15.

FESTIVAL HYMN.

To our own true Home,
This Thine House, we come,
Meet homage, as Thy children, here to pay:
Deeply grateful, we
Fain would "render Thee
Our thanks" for "benefits" renew'd each day.

"Thy most worthy praise"
On our festal days
With joy will we set forth, in duty bound,
When Thy servants meet
At Thy Mercy-seat
And tread with gladsome feet this holy ground.

When with one accord
"Thy Most Holy Word"
With rev'rent awe and filial love we hear,
That we may fulfil
In our lives Thy will,
Blest SPIRIT, grant to us the hearing ear.

LORD, vouchsafe to feed
In all time of need
Our souls and bodies in Paternal love,
And when life is o'er
May we aye adore
"Thy glorious Godhead" in the realms above.

Blessed TRINITY,
Mystic UNITY,
From out of Zion us Thy people cheer,
Shine forth in Thy might,
Be Thou our true Light,
Till we "before the GOD of gods" appear.

D

Choral Graces

BEFORE AND AFTER MEALS, AT FESTIVALS OF CHOIRS, Etc.

Set by Rev. J. B. Dykes, Mus. Doc.

Arranged to be sung as a Quartett, and repeated in Full Chorus.

GRACE BEFORE MEALS.

THOU, by Whom all creatures live,
Who dost our food and raiment give,
These gifts of Thine, Lord, sanctify,
As we Thy Name do glorify. Amen.

GRACE AFTER MEALS.

OR these and countless mercies be
All glory, Tri-une God, to Thee;
To serve Thee, Lord, our hearts incline,
Make body, soul, and spirit Thine.
Alleluia. Amen.

Dedication Festival Hymns.

* No. I.

SET TO MUSIC BY J. BAPTISTE CALKIN.

"Seek ye My face. Thy face, Lord, will I seek."

THOU, Who dwellest in eternity,
    Receive us as we consecrate to Thee
        This day of festal gladness.

For meet it is that we, the sons of earth,
Should seek our FATHER'S face in time of mirth
        And days of festal gladness.

One day amid Thy Courts is better far
Than thousand days, when these unhallow'd are
        Though days of festive gladness.

LORD, teach us of Thy sweetness here to taste,
Thine House shall then be sought with eager haste.
        To share true festal gladness.

Thy days shall then as pools of water be,
Thy people shall Thy power and glory see
        Amid their festal gladness.

Fit and prepare our earth-worn hearts to sing
The LAMB'S "New Song," and us Thy servants bring
        To endless festal gladness.   Amen.

---

* This and Hymns III. and IV. sung at the Re-opening of S. Thomas Church, Launceston, after Restoration. Contributed to Harland's Supplemental Hymns, and other Collections.

*No. II.

SET TO MUSIC BY DR. GAUNTLETT.

"Behold I lay in Zion, for a foundation, a stone, a tried stone, a precious corner-stone, a sure foundation."

IN humble adoration,
    We lift our souls to Thee,
    O CHRIST the Rock of Ages,
    With us Thy servants be;
In this and all our labours,
    Our efforts deign to bless;
Vouchsafe this work to prosper,
    And crown it with success.

Thou art the sure Foundation,
    The precious Corner-stone;
On Grace Divine depending,
    We rest on Thee alone.
Though winds and floods be raging,
    As in the stormy sea,
Our House shall stand securely,
    Sustained and built on Thee.

O grant us to be builded,
    As stones set in their place,
Part of Thy Church's fabric,
    Cemented by Thy Grace;
That when this earthly dwelling
    Shall crumble to the ground,
Our Heavenly habitation
    May then for aye be found.

---

* Written for the Laying the Foundation Stone of the New Grammar School, by Judge Haliburton, M.P. for Launceston, when the writer was Head Master.

DEDICATION FESTIVAL HYMNS.

To Thee, O King Eternal,
   Immortal SON, to Thee;
And Thee, O blessed SPIRIT,
   All praise ascribèd be
By us and all Thy people,
   In all their works begun,
Continuing, and ended,
   Whilst ages yet shall run.

No. III.

"I was glad when they said unto me, we will go into the House of the Lord."

LORD, we love the habitation
   Of Thy holy House below,
Blest abode of consolation
   In this vale of tears and woe;
     Alleluia, Alleluia,
For the grace Thou dost bestow.

Here we gain our early union
   With the one great family,
Here we join in sweet communion
   With the brotherhood and Thee.
     Alleluia, Alleluia,
To Thy Name all glory be.

In Thine House glad tidings greet us
   From the pages of Thy Word;
Promise, hope, and warning meet us,
   Waymarks these Thou dost afford,
     Alleluia, Alleluia,
For the truths our ears have heard.

Here we meet for preparation
For th' Eternal Courts above;
Here we yield Thee adoration,
FATHER, SON, and Heavenly DOVE,
Alleluia, Alleluia,
Three in One, we sing Thy love. Amen.

No. IV.

"The Lord shall comfort Zion, He shall comfort all her waste places."

COMFORTER of Zion's wastes,
Restorer of her ways,
Her walls when lying desolate
Thou dost in pity raise:
To-day with grateful strain,
O LORD our Righteousness,
This house renew'd again,
Thy sacred Name we bless.

Fulfil Thy promise, as of old,
To us assembled here,
And ever "be Thine ears attent"
Thy servants' prayer to hear:
Then we with grateful strain
O LORD our Righteousness,
This house renew'd again,
Thy sacred Name will bless.

Our hearts inspire with joyfulness,
As we Thy praises sing,
And deck Thy priests with holiness,
Thou great High Priest and King:

So all with grateful strain,
  O LORD our Righteousness,
This house renew'd again,
  Thy sacred Name shall bless.

O Trinity in Unity
  Thou FATHER of us all,
Thou SON of GOD and HOLY GHOST
  On Thee Thy people call:
And in our grateful strain
  To Thee our Righteousness,
We swell the loud refrain,
  Thy sacred Name to bless.

✠

* Morning.

"Looking for and hasting unto the coming of the day of God."
—2 S. PETER III. 12.

FRAMER of the light,
    Who from out the night
The dawn of joyous day again dost bring,
    On our darkened eyes
    Bid Thy bright beams rise,—
Of endless glory teach us, LORD, to sing.

    By Thy mercy still
    Spared our place to fill,
O FATHER, be it ours Thy Name to bless,
    Shelter'd by Thy power
    In each fleeting hour
Thy people guide to paths of holiness.

    Raised from death-like sleep
    Ever may we keep
Alive within us thoughts of that great day!
    Grant the ready mind,
    Give us grace to find
The strait gate unto life—the narrow way.

    Onward to the goal
    Lead each striving soul,
Upheld by strength Thy Grace Divine supplies;
    While it yet is day,
    May we win our way
"Towards the mark, and our high calling's prize."

---

* Set to music by Sir Jos. Barnby. Published in the Parish Church Hymnal. Also published in Mrs. Carey Brock's Children's Hymn Book, to music by J. B. Dykes, Mus. Doc.

Evening.

"Unto Thee, O Lord, do I lift up my soul."—PSALM XXV. 1.

LORD, it is a joyful thing
    To praise Thy glorious Name,
  In strains of thankfulness to sing,
    And all Thy truth proclaim—
Thy loving kindness each new morn,
  Thy faithfulness each night :
"Our House of refuge, Thou! the Horn
  Of our defence—our might."

Each day fresh mercies, gracious LORD,
  So undeserved, so great,
In bounteous love Thou dost afford :
  On Thee all eyes do wait
For life, and health, and precious hours,
  Salvation's work to speed—
For food and raiment—all the powers
  Supplied to each one's need.

Yet how unworthy, LORD, are we
  Of all Thy daily care !
We own in deep humility
  How cold at best we are.
O gentle JESU, bid us know
  Thy love, then, in return
Our earth-worn hearts anew shall glow,
  Our zeal afresh shall burn.

---

* Set to music by R. Minton Taylor. Published in the Parish Church Hymnal.

Each night our praises shall ascend
  Before Thy Mercy-seat :
With Thy prevailing Name shall blend
  Our prayers as incense sweet.
If through the mists of earth to Thee
  Our souls begin to rise,
"The lifting of our hands shall be
  An evening sacrifice." Amen.

*Sunday Morning.

"This is the day the Lord hath made; we will rejoice and be glad in it."—PSALM CXVIII. 24.

LORD of the New Creation,
    Of righteousness the Sun,
When Thou for our Salvation
    The victory hadst won,
Thou didst for sin-stained mortals
    On that first Easter morn,
Break through the tomb's dark portals,
    To life and light new-born.

This is the day Thou madest,
    With gladness we rejoice,
To greet Thee as Thou badest,
    We lift the heart and voice:
"Sons of the Resurrection,"
    And "children of the day,"
Thy grace and safe protection
    Vouchsafe to us we pray.

One day, good LORD, in seven
    To men, with toil opprest,
Thou hast in mercy given—
    Foretaste of endless rest,
"The rest that yet remaineth
    For all who shall be Thine";
This day Thy love ordaineth
    With Heavenly light shall shine.

---

* Set to music by E. H. Thorne. Published in the Parish Church Hymnal.

A halo still is resting
  As erst so long ago,
Its golden gleam investing
  These days with mystic glow;
Still doth Thy presence lighten
  This lower world of ours,
Those Easter rays still brighten
  Each Sunday's matin hours.

_{*} *This hymn may also be used on Easter Day.*

*Sunday Evening.

"Then the same day at evening, being the first day of the week, when the doors were shut . . . for fear of the Jews, came Jesus and stood in the midst, and saith unto them, Peace be unto you."
—S. JOHN XX. 19.

HOU, Who through shades of night
With flaming pillar bright
Israel's hosts didst light,
  JEHOVAH GOD!
Thy gracious guidance still
Need we 'gainst every ill,
To us Thy word fulfil,
  JEHOVAH GOD.

Thou, Who at eve didst stand
'Mid the disciples' band,
When danger seemed at hand,
  JESU our LORD.
As then, so now, O say
On this—the week's first day—
"Peace" to our souls, we pray,
  JESU our LORD.

Thou, Who with "fire of love"
Thy saint of old didst move,
Soft-breathing Heavenly Dove,
  Blest PARACLETE:
Thou, Who with light Divine
On that LORD'S Day didst shine, †
Pour on us gifts of Thine,
  Blest PARACLETE.

---

* Set to music by R. Minton Taylor. Published in the Parish Church Hymnal.

† "I was in the Spirit on the Lord's Day" (Rev. i. 10).

SUNDAY EVENING.

Most Holy TRINITY,
In mystic Unity,
Hear while we call on Thee,
    Dread THREE in ONE:
With us at Eventide
On Thine own Day abide,
Thy people guard and guide,
    Dread THREE in ONE. Amen.

Final Hymns for Sunday Evening.

No. I.

"Thine eyes shall see the King in His beauty: they shall behold the land that is very far off."

WE strangers are and pilgrims,
   As all our fathers were,
  To that far distant country
   We sojourners repair;
We journey ever onward
   Until we reach that bourne
Awaiting all the living,
   Whence none may e'er return.

We strangers are and pilgrims
   'Mid scenes of toil and care:
And here are strife and sorrow,
   But peace and joy are there
Where death can reign no longer
   Nor tempter may molest,
The wicked cease from troubling,
   The weary are at rest.

We strangers are and pilgrims,
   Our Sundays, one by one,
Are gliding swiftly past us,
   The goal is not yet won,—
Lo! now the time accepted!
   Lo! now Salvation's day!
Too late may be the morrow
   If still in sin we stray.

We strangers are and pilgrims,
　　This earth is not our home:
With no abiding city,
　　We seek for one to come:
O JESU safely bring us
　　To that far distant land
Where Thou in beauty reignest
　　Amid Thine Angel band. Amen.

No. II.

" Behold the day groweth to an end."

LORD, once more Thy Day is done,
　　Of all days the first and best,
One more week with Thee begun,
　　On this Day of peace and rest.
JESU, take us to Thy keeping,
Guard us waking, guard us sleeping.

When our prayers and alms we bring
　　Unto Thee in Whom we live,
Deign to bless each offering,
　　All our wand'ring thoughts forgive.
JESU, take us to Thy keeping,
Guard us waking, guard us sleeping.

Now our sacred prayers are said,
　　Sung are all our hymns of praise,
From Thy Word each lesson read,
　　Yet one final strain we raise—
JESU, take us to Thy keeping
Guard us waking, guard us sleeping.

Known to Thee is each one's need,
  Help from Thee Thy servants seek
All their daily course to speed—
  Shield us through the coming week.
JESU, take us to Thy keeping,
Guard us waking, guard us sleeping. Amen.

"*The Lord Himself is thy Keeper.*"

No. III.

"*My Peace give I unto you, not as the world giveth give I unto you.*"

LORD, ere Thy Day be o'er,
  Grant us Thy Peace:
Hear Thou our cry once more,
  Grant us Thy Peace.
'Mid care and toil and strife,
  All through this changeful life,
With deep unrest so rife,
  Grant us Thy Peace.

Ere yet Thine House we leave,
  Grant us Thy Peace:
Lest we Thy SPIRIT grieve,
  Grant us Thy Peace.
Thy promised help we claim,
  Keep us from sin and shame,
We pray in JESU'S Name
  Grant us Thy Peace.

Thy Days will soon be done,
  Grant us Thy Peace:
And our short course be run,
  Grant us Thy Peace.

Ere to the world we turn,
  Make our cold hearts to burn
Life-giving truth to learn,
  Grant us Thy Peace.

Our drooping spirits cheer,
  Grant us Thy Peace :
In time of need be near,
  Grant us Thy Peace.
Thine HOLY SPIRIT give,
  In Whom alone we live :
All our misdeeds forgive,
  And grant us Peace. Amen.

* No. IV.

"At evening time it shall be light."

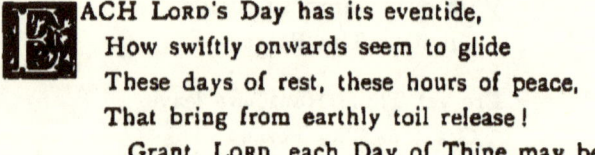ACH LORD'S Day has its eventide,
  How swiftly onwards seem to glide
  These days of rest, these hours of peace,
  That bring from earthly toil release !
    Grant, LORD, each Day of Thine may be
    A foretaste of our rest in Thee.

It is Thine Own Day's eventide,
Throughout this week with us abide,
O be our Comfort, Guide, and Stay,
'Mid dangers that beset life's way :
  And thus each Day of Thine shall be,
  A foretaste of our rest in Thee.

---

* Printed in the Home Hymn Book.

FINAL HYMNS FOR SUNDAY EVENING. 67

Thy Day declines to eventide,
We leave Thy Courts—yet by our side
We need Thee—Guardian of our life,
To shield us in the daily strife,
   To cause each Day of Thine to be
   A foretaste of our rest in Thee.

Let there be light at eventide,
Within each soul, though all beside
Be dark around—with Thee is light,*
O sanctify us all this night,
   For only thus Thy Day can be,
   Sweet foretaste of our rest in Thee. Amen.

† No. V.

"*For the Lord will go before you, and the God of Israel will be your Rereward.*"

ORD, ‡ prevent us in our doings
   With the fulness of Thy grace,
Ever in Thy service cheer us
   With the brightness of Thy face:
     So Thy children, with Thee nigh,
     Thy great Name shall glorify.

In our week-day work be with us,
   Each one's portion is from Thee.
Unto Thee we look to bless us,
   And our Staff and Stay to be;
     So Thy children, with Thee nigh,
     Thy great Name shall glorify.

---

* Psalm xxxvi. 9.   † Set to an Ancient Church Melody.
‡ Founded on the Church Collect, "Prevent us, O Lord," etc.

In all works begun and ended
  In Thee, while brief life shall last
Further us with help continued
  Till all dangers shall be past ;
    So Thy children, with Thee nigh,
    Thy great Name shall glorify.

When at last with sin and evil
  There shall be no longer strife,
Bring us JESU, in Thy mercy,
  To Thine Home of light and life;
    So with Thee for ever nigh,
    We Thy Name shall glorify. Amen.

HYMNS FOR CHURCH SEASONS.

Advent Hymns.

WRITTEN FOR A SERVICE OF SONG ENTITLED
"ADVENT-TIDE."

Placed on the Catalogue of S.P.C.K. Edited by the Author and A. H. Brown.

No. I.

Dire and Awful were the Judgments.

DIRE and awful were the judgments
    Thou, O LORD, didst once foretell,
Signs Thou gavest—all unheeded
    By unwatchful Israel.

As a hen her brood doth gather
    'Neath the shelter of her wing,
So wouldst Thou Thy wayward people,
    Safely through all dangers bring:

Of Thy warning words unmindful
    All unmoved by love or fear,
Of their promised King forgetful,
    Till in wrath Thou didst appear.

JESU, by their doom remind us
    Of our Visitation Day;
Grant us grace to seek and find Thee
    Ere it close and pass away.

No. II.
Pilgrims unto Zion.

PILGRIMS unto Zion,
    Watch, stand fast, be strong,
For the roaring lion
    Lurks the road along;
Up! life's night is waning,
    And the dawn is near,
Ye must ground be gaining
    Ere the Judge appear.

'Tis high time to waken
    From your slumbers deep,
One more year is taken;
    Rouse ye, then, from sleep:
Nearer is salvation,
    Near the awful day;
Now the works of darkness
    Ye must cast away.

Walk ye all uprightly
    As in day's broad light,
When it shineth brightly,
    Not as in the night;
Not in drunken riot,
    Not in wanton lust,
Not in strife's disquiet,
    Not in ways unjust.

Put ye on the raiment
    Of GOD'S Own dear SON,—
Robes by costly payment
    He for you hath won:
Of Him be our praises,
    These our life-long strain—
Such His Church still raises,
    Till He come again. Amen.

No. III.

In their Master's Name.

IN their Master's Name
    Heralds now proclaim—
"Soon this world shall be no more,
Soon this fleeting life be o'er;
    Children of the day,
    Ye must watch and pray."

    LORD, Thy pastors bless:
    Clothed with righteousness,
With fresh zeal their love renew;
With Thy sevenfold gifts endue,
    So men's hearts shall burn
    As to Thee they turn.

    To prepare the road
    For the SON OF GOD
One in days of old was sent
Bidding all men to repent:
    May Thine heralds still
    This Thy Word fulfil.

No. IV.
Time's Course Ever Onward.

TIME'S course ever onward
  So noiselessly steals:
Ere long shall be nearing
  His chariot wheels;
'Mid hosts He is coming
  On clouds in the sky:
Every eye shall behold Him—
  His Advent is nigh:
    Far spent is the night,
      Close at hand is the day;
    Clad in armour of light,
      Darksome deeds put away.

Speeds on that dread Advent,
  Its tokens abound,
While warning notes utter
  Their ominous sound
As leaves on the fig-tree
  When summer is nigh,
The Parable's teaching
  Faith's glance can descry.
    Far spent, &c.

Up! let us be stirring,
  Up! wake out of sleep,
The Church and her members
  Their vigils must keep:
The judgment is nearer,
  As closes each year,
The Judge is approaching
  Full soon to appear.
    Far spent, &c.

Hymns, etc., from "Christmas-tide,"

A SERVICE OF SACRED SONG.*

No. I.
Mid Gross Darkness.

MID gross darkness earth was lying,
    Deep the gloom o'er ev'ry clime,
    Ere the Day-Star had arisen—
    Long expected—"late in time,"
Jesu, we behold Thee come
From Thine high and Heavenly Home.

In the latter days appearing,
    Through long ages dimly seen,
    In the bosom of the Father
    His Belovèd Thou hadst been.
    Jesu, we behold, &c.

Though no palace be Thy birthplace,
    Cradled in no royal state;
    Though no earthly pomp or splendour
    Round Thy Virgin-Mother wait;
    Jesu, we behold, &c.

Offspring of the meek and lowly,
    Of the meek the Meekest Thou;
    Let all nations hail Thine advent,
    Let all knees before Thee bow.
    Jesu, we behold, &c.

---

* Placed with others on the Supplemental Catalogue of the S.P.C.K.

No. II.

Raise the Strain of High Thanksgiving.

RAISE the strain of high thanksgiving,
    Glory, laud, and honour sing,
Unto JESUS, GOD Incarnate—
    Babe of earth, of Heaven the King:
In the highest be all glory,
    Peace on earth, goodwill to men.

Wondrous truth, all truths excelling,
    In the flesh GOD manifest;
Taking manhood into Godhead,
    Great the mystery confest:
In the highest be all glory,
    Peace on earth, goodwill to men.

"Heir of all things" was appointed
    He by Whom the worlds were made;
Brightness of His FATHER's glory,
    Love amazing has displayed:
In the highest be all glory,
    Peace on earth, goodwill to men.

Angels from on high adore Him,
    Now His lowly birth proclaim;
Come, and let us bow before Him,
    As we praise His holy Name:
In the highest be all glory,
    Peace on earth, goodwill to men.

No. III.

Pastorale.

JESU, on this blessèd morn
Thou in Bethlehem wast born;
Once again we turn to see
Mercy meeting truth in Thee.
When, blest SAVIOUR, Thou didst come
From Thine high and Heavenly Home,
Thou from sin didst bring release,
Joining righteousness with peace.
   Jesu, on this blessèd morn
   Thou in Bethlehem wast born.

They of old, 'mid darkness drear,
Did the songs of Angels hear;
While, amid the gloom of night,
Brightly shone that wondrous light,
Gentle JESU, now we raise
Feeble notes of grateful praise
As we tell that tale again,
As we sing that sweetest strain.
   Jesu, on this blessèd morn
   Thou in Bethlehem wast born.

Help us glory best to give
By the CHRIST-like lives we live;
Learning thus of "peace on earth"
From the story of Thy birth.
On the good and evil still
Thou dost cause Thy sun to shine;
May we strive to show good will
Unto all, for we are Thine.
   Jesu, on this blessèd morn
   Thou in Bethlehem wast born.

No. IV.
*All Hail! All Hail!

ALL hail! all hail to the natal day
  Of the Lord of life and glory !
Your homage bring to the Infant King,
  As ye chant the wondrous story.
    To Bethlehem! To Bethlehem!
      Is the way we now are wending;
    To Jesus, born in Bethlehem,
      Are the thoughts of all hearts tending.

Age follows age in a ceaseless round,
  Since the Angels' midnight greeting;
Men live and die—but the Church for aye
  Is at Christmas-tide repeating:
    To Bethlehem, &c.

Then come and awake your tuneful strain,
  As ye sing in exultation;
Come, bear your part with a grateful heart
  In this Day's commemoration.
    To Bethlehem, &c.

Yes, onward, ye Christians, onward move,
  On to Bethlehem to meet Him ;
With reverent mirth, O ye Sons of Earth,
  As your GOD Incarnate greet Him.
    To Bethlehem, &c.

---

* Set to music by E. H. Thorne. Printed in the Parish Hymnal, and reprinted in the Christmas-tide Service of Song.

Hymns for Passion-tide and the Lenten Season.

No. I.

As now before the Mind.

"To know the love of Christ which passeth knowledge."

S now before the mind
    Thoughts of Thy Passion rise,
    The wondrous worth our spirits find
    Of Love's dread sacrifice!
O JESU, as Thy pains we ponder o'er,
Our hearts inflame, that we may learn to love Thee more.

    No thought can fully reach,
    No tongue proclaim so well,
    The love Thy Cross alone can teach—
    Its marvels who may tell—
That Thou shouldst leave for us Thy throne on high—
For us, the sinful sons of men, to agonize and die?

    JESU, be with us now,
    While once again is told
    The story of Thy Cross, and how
    Thou didst Thy love unfold:
And while Thy pains and grief we ponder o'er
In godly sorrow, may we learn to love Thee more.

---

* Published by Pitman, in a Service of Song in two parts, suitable for the "Three Hours'" Service containing the Narrative of the Passion from the Four Gospels.

No. II.

Say, Who is This?

"Thou wentest forth for the salvation of Thy people, even for salvation with Thine Anointed."—HAB. III. 13.

AY, who is this? Hosannas loud
Arise from out the surging crowd;
"The Prophet JESUS cometh—
He of Nazareth of Galilee!"

Thy King of Whom the prophets speak,
To Thee, O Zion, cometh "meek";
And, long expected—lo! at length
Is here, "in greatness of His strength."

To Thee the children fitly sing,
For of the child-like Thou art King;
The meek and lowly learn of Thee—
Of such Thy Kingdom, LORD, shall be.

Ride on! with blood those garments dyed,
As prophet's vision erst descried:—
Thy "little ones," their conflict o'er,
The LAMB shall follow evermore.

✢

No. III.

In a Garden once when Tempted.

"Thou that dwellest in the gardens, the companions hearken to Thy voice—cause me to hear it."—SONG OF SOLOMON VIII. 13.

IN a garden once when tempted
   "Adam by transgression fell,"—
Fitly Thou—the Second Adam
   In a garden didst repel
Satan and his powers of evil,
   In Thy might invincible.

In a garden once was eaten
   Pleasant food that seemèd good;
In a garden CHRIST, our Adam,
   Drain'd the bitter cup, and stood
Champion in the direful struggle,
   Victor in the deadly feud.

When from Eden's garden driven
   Adam heard sin's penalty,
"Sweat of brow" was then his portion;
   But in dire Gethsemane,
From the LORD that curse undoing,
   "Sweat of blood" there needs must be.

In a garden once the sentence
   Unto death on all began,
Stretching o'er successive ages
   With its dread and darksome ban,—
In a garden spent its fury,
   Borne by Thee, the SON OF MAN.

✠

No. IV.

Holy Jesu, when in Grief.

"What! could ye not watch with Me one hour?"

HOLY JESU, when in grief
  Thy disciples sought relief,
  Thrice o'ercome by slumber brief—
    Thou didst gently chide them:
So Thy people humbly pray
Thou wouldst check them when they stray,
Watching o'er them by the way,
    That no ill betide them.

Oft-times when we fail to learn,
Thou in mercy dost "return,"
While our hearts within us burn,
    As Thou dost reprove us.
Grant that in our time of need
We Thy gentle voice may heed,
And may follow if Thou lead,
    Should Thy SPIRIT move us.

What if now Thou art on high,
Still to Thee we may draw nigh,
By Thy mystic agony
    With the FATHER pleading:
Hear whene'er we call on Thee,
Advocate for us to be,
With Thy FATHER'S majesty
    Ever interceding.

✠

No. V.
O Saviour Mine.

"Keep back Thy servant also from presumptuous sins, lest they get the dominion over me."

SAVIOUR mine,
  The traitor's sign—
Pretence of love—betrayed Thee;
O keep Me from false-heartedness,
  Oft have I disobeyed Thee.

O JESU, meek,
  When foes did seek
With dark intent to bind Thee:
Thyself didst e'en to them make known;
  My JESUS, may I find Thee.

Thy mighty word
  The soldiers heard,
And straightway fell before Thee;
O cast Thou down my stubborn will,
  And cause me to adore Thee.

Thy chosen Thou
  Didst then allow
In terror to forsake Thee;
Restrain me by Thy grace and power,
  That I *my* LORD may make Thee.
        Amen.

* No. VI.

See the Guiltless Captive.

EE the guiltless Captive standing,
    Mocked and smitten—put to shame !
Hear His recreant Apostle
    His dear Master now disclaim !

Yet again His LORD denying—
    Where is now his boasted zeal ?
Challeng'd as a Galilean—
    Curse and oath the man reveal.

See His gentle Master turning
    One sad look reproachfully.
Hark ! he hears the note of warning—
    Weeping then so bitterly.

Godly sorrow, JESU, grant us,
    May a tender look from Thee
Melt the stony heart within us,
    Ere Thou come our Judge to be.

---

* Written to music sung by the Jews, at their wailing place in Jerusalem.

No. VII.

Behold the Man.

BEHOLD the Man!
  Man for us men—
 To purchase our salvation
  Thou camest forth to be,
  'Mid scorn and mockery,
An "Outcast" and "Rejected" of the nation.

  Behold the Man!
  Man for us men—
 Lord Jesu, we behold Thee
  Now standing by the throne,
  There pleading for Thine own,
As erst for those "who set at nought and sold Thee."

  Behold the Man!
  Man for us men—
 Dear title by Thee taken!
  O "Son of Man," we pray
  Ever to us display
Thy wondrous love—and ours for Thee awaken.

  Behold the Man!
  Man for us men—
 Emmanuel we hail Thee!
  Father, behold Thy Son—
  Jesu, Who life hast won,
In weeping for our sins, we best bewail Thee.*

---

* "Daughters of Jerusalem, weep not for Me, but weep for yourselves, and for your children."

No. VIII.

Lo! the Cross is Raised on High.

LO! the Cross is raised on high,
Hark! they rail—those passers-by.
Dire the load of grief and scorn,
Holy JESU, Thou hast borne.

SOLO. *"Is it nothing to you, all ye that pass by?—
Behold and see if there be any sorrow like unto My sorrow."* *

Lo! a Name is written there,
None in all the earth so fair
As upon Thy Cross is seen,
JESUS—KING—the NAZARENE.

SOLO—*Is it nothing, &c.*

Ah! that thirst—that thorny crown!
Those red drops that trickle down;
In that cry what agony,
"Why hast Thou forsaken Me?"

SOLO—*Is it nothing, &c.*

"It is finished," hear Him say,
Ere His Spirit passed away;
Mighty Victor in the strife,
By Thy death Thou givest life.

---

* Lamentations i. 12.

No. IX.

O Thou, Who for Man's Sake.

"Looking unto Jesus, the Author and Finisher of our faith."

 THOU, Who for man's sake
    Didst blessedness forego,
Our human flesh on Thee to take,
    And life of woe.
That precious life begun
    With toil and ceaseless strain,
Must close, ere yet its course be run,
    In sharpest pain.

Salvation to procure
    Thou didst the work begin;
Upheld by Thee may we endure
    And conquer sin.
Of faith the Author Thou—
    By sacrifice so vast;
As Finisher we seek Thee now,
    While life shall last.

Redeemer, by Thy life,
    O teach us how to live,
Sustain us—'mid the earthly strife
    Thy succour give.
Thou Who our flesh hast worn,
    When our last hour is nigh,
Then by Thy Cross so meekly borne,
    Teach us to die. Amen.

*Hymn for Good Friday.

"What shall I render unto the Lord for all the benefits He hath done unto me?"

DARK and dreary day,
  When JESUS died to pay
    Sin's awful penalty!
The sun kept back his light
To hide that mournful sight
    When JESUS died for me.

Ah! who can tell those pangs
As on the Cross He hangs,
    My dearest LORD, for me?
For me He dies that death,
For me He yields His breath
    My sinful soul to free.

And as He bows His head,
Have I no tears to shed?
    When I look back and see
Those loving arms spread wide
To draw me to His side—
    My ransom thus to be?

O JESU, may Thy love
My strength and succour prove,
    That I to Thee may live.
Thou gavest all for me,
May I devote to Thee
    What little I can give. Amen.

---

* Printed in a Supplemental Hymnal edited by Lady Victoria Freke, and set to music by A. H. Brown, Rev. J. B. Dykes, Mus. Doc., Canon F. A. J. Hervey, and W. Macfarren. Also in "The Home and School Hymnal," Free Church of Scotland, to music by Dr. Vincent and by H. J. Trembath. Printed in the Hymnal of the United Presbyterian Churches of Scotland and Ireland.

O God Most High, Most Holy.

"The sacrifices of God are a broken spirit: a broken and a contrite heart, O God, Thou wilt not despise."—PSALM LI. 17.

GOD most High, most Holy,
    No mortal eye may see
    Thy dread mysterious dwelling,
      Thine awful Majesty.
Thy ways are not as our ways,
    Thy footsteps are unknown,
Exalted far above us
    On Thine Eternal Throne.

Wherewith shall we adore Thee?
    What presents can we bring?
Or how appear before Thee
    With votive offering?
One gift we all can offer,
    And precious in Thine eyes—
"A broken, contrite spirit,
    LORD, Thou wilt not despise."

Though high above all heavens,
    On earth Thou lovest well
With us, unworthy servants,
    O FATHER, here to dwell.
To all Thy waiting people
    Thy saving grace impart;
For JESU'S sake, O give us
    The lowly contrite heart. Amen.

For Lent, Holy Week, Good Friday, or at Missions.

The Sinner's Urgent Needs—
*Pardon, Peace, Power.

Written to the music of 322, Hymns A. and M.

PARDON.—The Petition.

"*Thou art a God ready to pardon, gracious and merciful, slow to anger, and of great kindness.*"—Nehemiah IX. 17.

"*Thou, Lord, art good, ready to forgive; and plenteous in mercy to all who call upon Thee.*"—Psalm LXXXVI. 5.

O GREAT Absolver,† Thou, Who didst commend
    Thy love to lost mankind while yet in sin,
    Much more to us, Thy pardon wilt extend,
    Brought nigh by blood of Jesus, Who, to win
Our souls from death, and in our utmost need
By Thee unspar'd, did as the Victim bleed.

The Promise.

"*Let him return unto the Lord . . . He will abundantly pardon.*"
—Isaiah LV. 7.
"*I will pardon all their iniquities, whereby they have sinned.*"
—Jeremiah XXXIII. 8.

"SEEK ye the Lord while yet He may be found,
    Call ye upon Him while He still is near."
    "The riches of His grace" ‡ shall aye abound,
    And to repentant prodigals appear.
"Return" all ye who have done wickedly,
His pardon ye shall have abundantly.

---

* "There are three things which every thoughtful man who views himself in the presence of God, and as a traveller to Eternity, must realize that he needs, and they are Pardon, Peace, and Power."—*Bishop of Exeter.*

    † Romans v. 8.   ‡ Ephesians i. 7-8.

PEACE.—THE PETITION.

"Grant us Thy peace."
"Give peace in our time, O Lord."—PRAYER BOOK.

NOT only pardon—grant us, LORD, Thy peace,
    While " we draw near with boldness to Thy
        Throne," *
And from accusing conscience give release ;
    Nor us, Thy sons, though erring sons, disown.
Thou, Who Thy SON to be our Peace didst give,
Wilt Thou not bid His peace within us live?

THE PROMISE.

"I will give peace and quietness unto Israel."—1 CHRON. XXII. 9.
"Peace I leave with you, My peace I give unto you."
        —S. JOHN XIV. 27.

MY peace I left for you, My peace I gave—
    Not as the world doth give, give I to you—
    " Ye tribulation in the world must have,"
    Be of good cheer—My peace I will renew.
† " Peace, perfect peace in this dark world of sin—
My blood to you shall whisper peace within."

---

* Hebrews iv. 16 *(Revised Version)*.

† " From Year to Year "—Evening Hymn, by the Bishop of Exeter.

POWER.—The Petition.

"*Be not Thou far from me, O Lord: O my Strength, haste Thee to help me.*"—PSALM XXII. 19.

"*O Lord, raise up, we pray Thee, Thy power and come among us, and with great might succour us.*"—PRAYER BOOK.

    YET once again, O FATHER, do we plead—
        Not only peace and pardon, LORD, bestow,
    "But by 'Thine everlasting love,' our need
        'Mid perils of our warfare here below
    Supply, and 'day by day, yea hour by hour,'
    * Vouchsafe to us Thy blessed SPIRIT'S power."

THE PROMISE.

"*He giveth power to the faint; and to them that have no might He increaseth strength.*"—ISAIAH XL. 29.

"*Ye shall receive power,* after that the Holy Ghost is come upon you.*"—ACTS I. 8.

    "TURN you at My reproof, and then—Behold
        I will pour out My SPIRIT unto you," †
    With all His might and graces manifold,
    And you—so "strengthless for the fight" ‡—renew.
    "Your GOD am I from all the ages past,
    Your GOD to be while endless ages last."

---

* "The special gift of the SPIRIT which he mentions is *power*."—*Bishop How's Commentary*.

† Proverbs i. 23.

‡ "Infirma nostri corporis
    Virtute firmans perpeti."
Ancient Latin Hymn, re-translated by the Bishop of Exeter. Whitsun Day—"From Year to Year."

Easter Hymns from "Easter-tide,"

A SERVICE OF SONG.

ALL THE SONG-SERVICES EDITED BY THE AUTHOR AND
A. H. BROWN.

* No. I.

The Sheaf of First-fruits at Thy Word.

THE sheaf of First-fruits at Thy word
In olden days they brought,
To wave before the Harvest's LORD,
With mystic meaning fraught.

We render homage unto Thee,
Who art the Living Bread—
Who didst vouchsafe for us to be
"The First-fruits of the dead."

When from the furrows of the grave
Earth shall its full ears yield,
May we amid the wheat-corn wave
In that last Harvest-field.   Amen.

---

* Set to music by A. H. Brown.

*No. II.

Christ is Risen from the Dead.

CHRIST is risen from the dead,
     Alleluia!
Of His Church High Priest and Head,
     Alleluia!
Who corruption could not see,
     Alleluia!
Nor of death could holden be,
     Alleluia!

When He rose on that third day,
     Alleluia!
Sin and Satan vanquished lay,
     Alleluia!
Life for mortals He began,
     Alleluia!
"Tasting death for every man,"
     Alleluia!

First-fruits of our fallen race,
     Alleluia!
Brightness of the FATHER'S face,
     Alleluia!
All who sleep beneath Thy wing,
     Alleluia!
GOD ere long with Him shall bring,
     Alleluia!

On this glorious Day of days,
     Alleluia!
Strains of triumph we would raise,
     Alleluia!
Death and grave, O LORD, to Thee
     Alleluia!
Needs must yield the victory,
     Alleluia! Amen.

---

* Music by Rev. Canon F. A. J. Hervey, Chaplain to H.R.H. the Prince of Wales.

*No. III.

Uplift your hearts, exult as ye sing.

    UPLIFT your hearts, exult as ye sing
        Of your LORD over death victorious;
    Now He lives on high never more to die,
        Come and sing of His triumph glorious.
    Uplift your hearts, exult as ye sing
        Of your LORD over death victorious.

O death, where now is thy sting so dire?
    And thy thraldom, O grave, that bound us?
Evermore in strife will the LORD of life
    Cast the arm of His might around us.
        Uplift your hearts, &c.

We take our rest in the grave in peace,
    For the Captain of our salvation
Has achieved to-day for His Church alway
    Of her life this the Consummation.
        Uplift your hearts, &c.

In strains of joy holy anthems raise,
    Of His might and His mercy sing ye
Highest notes of praise on this Day of days,
    And your best of oblations bring ye.
        Uplift your hearts, &c.

---

   * Music composed for this Hymn by Sir John Stainer, M.A., Mus. Doc.

✠

Hymns, etc., for Ascension-tide.

No. I.

Remote, in Distant Days.

REMOTE, in distant days,
    A glorious truth portending,
Elijah borne aloft,
    Type of the LORD ascending,
Proclaims, in accents clear,
    To ages yet to come,
The Great High Priest's return
    To His eternal home.

Lo! parting now from earth,
    His mantle he is leaving;
His Master's spirit thus
    Elisha is receiving;
So JESU for Thy Church
    Thou gracious gifts hast left,
Not wholly comfortless,
    Nor of Thy grace bereft.*

The prophet long they sought
    In vain, with awe and wonder,
The ties that bound to earth
    Henceforth were cut asunder.
So from the things of time
    And life's depressing ways,
JESU, ascended LORD,
    Our hearts, we pray Thee, raise. Amen.

---

* "I will not leave you comfortless" (orphans).

No. II.

Lo, Heaven's Gates Unfolding.

    LO, heaven's gates unfolding,
      And everlasting doors,
    Hark, how the strain of triumph
      The heavenly host outpours!
The King of Glory hail they—
  "The mighty LORD and strong."
"The LORD in battle mighty,"
  The burden of their song.

In His apparel glorious,
  His raiment stained with blood;
Of crimson dye His vesture,
  That tells of foes withstood.
"In righteousness He speaketh,"
  And "mighty, now to save,"
The Vanquisher all-potent
  Of hell, and death, and grave.

"Who is the King of Glory?"
  Demand they once again:
"The LORD GOD of Sabàoth,"
  Replies th' angelic train;
He is the King of Glory:
  Lift up your heads, ye gates,
Ye portals everlasting,
  On Him all glory waits.

✠

No. III.
The Psalmist's Questions.

"Who shall ascend into the hill of the LORD?"

CHOIR AND PEOPLE.
    Even he whose hands are cleansèd;
    Even he, whose heart is pure;
    He, "REFINER'S fire" abiding
    Shall endure.

"Who shall rise up in His holy place?"

CHOIR AND PEOPLE.
    He whose mind hath not been lifted
    Unto vanity around:
    By redeeming mercy standing
    Shall be found.

"LORD, who shall dwell in Thy tabernacle?"

CHOIR AND PEOPLE.
    He whose life is uncorrupted,
    Speaking truth and doing right,
    Neither harmful nor deceitful
    In GOD's sight.

"Who shall rest upon Thy holy hill?"

CHOIR AND PEOPLE.
    Who his MASTER's footstep seeketh,
    Lowly, kindly unto all;
    Whoso such as these things doeth—
    Shall not fall.

✠

No. IV.
To Purchase Man's Salvation.

TO purchase man's salvation
    Thou camest, LORD, to earth,
To raise his fallen nature,
    To give him second birth,
To be a "Man of Sorrows,"
    To die a death of pain,
Ere to Thy FATHER's bosom
    Thou didst return again.
      Blessing, honour, glory,
        To GOD gone up on high;
      Their songs of praise His people raise
        His Name to magnify.

And alway interceding
    Our great High Priest art Thou,
Within the "Place Most Holy"
    Thy people see Thee now.
Rich gifts for men receiving
    Thou sendest from above;
Enkindling by Thy SPIRIT
    Our Faith, and Hope, and Love.
      Blessing, honour, glory, &c.

An anchor sure and steadfast
    Shall be our hope in Thee;
Within the veil it enters,
    Our refuge there to be,
Melchisedek Thine order,
    By GOD's unchanging vow;
Thou dost with benediction
    Thy Church for aye endow.
      Blessing, honour, glory, &c. Amen.

Whitsun-tide Hymn.

O SPIRIT, all pervading,
   Proceeding from above,
Who through the vast creation
   With wondrous power dost move,
In Air, and Fire, and Water,
   Those elements of might—
In forces trine we view Thee
   Revealed by Sound and Sight.

With these the great Creator
   Doth cleanse and purify,
By these, O Blessed SPIRIT,
   Is seen Thine agency.
Thou workest as Thou willest,
   Apart from mortal ken,
The spirit-world Thy temple,
   Built of the souls of men.

Thus, bloweth "where it listeth"
   The Wind with fitful sound,
Whence coming, whither going,
   By none can e'er be found.
With Water Thou dost cleanse us,
   By Thee the mystic Birth—
Be Thou the "Springing Water"
   In us the sons of earth.

Thine, too, the Fire that cleanseth,
   Whose flame is Love and Light,
From dross the gold it purgeth,
   The dull it maketh bright.
O may we never grieve Thee,
   Nor quench Thy cleansing fire,
O still our earth-worn spirits,
   With life and love inspire.

Flower Service Hymns.

FROM "SPRING AND SUMMER-TIDE,"
A Service of Sacred Song.

*No. I.
Gracious Lord of all Creation.

GRACIOUS Lord of all creation,
    Hear us while we sing Thy praise,
Fill our souls with veneration
    For Thy wondrous works and ways,
        Earth, and air, and sea, and sky,
        Thee, Creator, glorify!

Thou art He Who earth arrayest
    In her garb of changeful hue;
Thou such matchless skill displayest
    In yon Heaven's arch of blue.
        Earth, and air, &c.

Countless forms with life are teeming,
    O'er the land and in the deep;
Endless tints of colour gleaming
    In each glen, and dale, and steep.
        Earth, and air, &c.

Tokens of Thy love surround us;
    Ever give us eyes to see
Beauty everywhere around us,
    Teaching, mighty God of Thee.
        Earth, and air, &c.

---

* Set to music by A. H. Brown.

* No. II.

To Thine House we Come.

TO Thine House we come,
  Children to their home,
Thy fairest gifts to man we gladly bring,
  While before Thee now
  We Thy people bow,
Of Thy creative skill, O GOD, we sing.

  Thou dost tint the flowers,
  'Mid earth's countless bowers:
Thy wisdom and their love their blooms display;
  Garb so fair and bright,
  Beauteous to the sight,
Not Solomon in glory did array.

  Thou dost bid the field
  Treasures thus to yield,
Fraught with deep lessons of a love Divine;
  Nurslings of the soil
  Neither " spin nor toil,"
For thus to clothe the fading grass is Thine.

---

* To music by Rev. J. B. Dykes, Mus. Doc.

*No. III.

Gifts for Mortals' Gladness.

IFTS for mortals' gladness
God the Giver gave;
Solace in their sadness
All His children have:
Yet, like life's short day,
So they pass away.

Flowers fading ever,
This their lesson teach : †
Ties of earth must sever,
Troubles all will reach;
Brief the joys of earth,
Fleeting all its mirth.

Vain the hopes we cherish
Fixed on time and sense,
Mocking while they perish,
Swiftly speeding hence:
Like those blooms so bright
Fading from our sight.

God by these hath spoken—‡
He would have us learn
Thus, by many a token,
To *those* joys to turn
On th' eternal shore,
Fading nevermore.

---

* Set to music by Rev. F. J. Hervey, Chaplain to H.R.H. the Prince of Wales.

† Job. xiv. 2.   ‡ S. James i. 10, 11.

*No. IV.

Unto Flow'rets Fair.

UNTO flow'rets fair
    Wisdom doth compare
  Thee, the Bride on earth abiding,
'Neath the Bridegroom's shelter hiding:
    Thee His spouse we hail,
    †Lily of the Vale!

    To His promise true,
    Sends He gentle dew,
  To thy life fresh vigour lending,
O'er thy wide-spread roots descending:
    †Rose of Sharon thou,
    His beloved now!

    House of GOD Most High,
    Thee to beautify
  Bring we floral gifts the rarest,
Sprays the choicest, blooms the fairest,
    With our songs of praise
    On Thy festal days.

---

* Set to music by A. H. Brown.

† "I am the Rose of Sharon, and the Lily of the Valleys."—*Canticles ii.* 1.

*No. V.

The Merciful and Gracious Lord.

PSALM CXI. 4; AND LXVI. 2; 1 TIM. VI. 17.

"THE merciful and gracious LORD hath so done His marvellous works, that they ought to be had in remembrance. Say unto GOD, O how wonderful art Thou in Thy works. The living GOD, Who giveth us richly all things to enjoy."

CHORUS.

Alleluia to Thee for the sunny hours
Of the balmy Spring, and the Summer flowers;
For the genial rain from the clouds above:
So Thou visitest earth with Thy gifts of love.
Alleluia to Thee, for 'mid scenes of woe,
Thou vouchsafest sweet tokens to all below
Of that glorious Land far beyond the skies,
Of those flowers that are fairest in Paradise.
Amen.

* Music by J. B. Dykes.

*No. VI.

Because the Sick and Poor.

BECAUSE the sick and poor
  Are Jesu's tender care,
These gifts from out our humble store
  With gladness we prepare.

Amid those weary hours
  Spent on the couch of pain,
Amid the sickness that devours
  Men's strength with ceaseless drain:

These flowers their message bring,
  In all their bright array;
While thoughts and hearts they help to wing
  To Heaven's changeless day.

No gift, however small,
  We give to Thine for Thee,
Shall ever prove in vain, but all
  As store shall treasured be.

O Jesu, in Thy Name
  The cup of water given,
Or widow's mite, shall surely claim
  Reward from Thee in Heaven.

Write Thou in each one's heart
  How unto gifts for Thee
A priceless worth Thy words impart:
  "YE DID IT UNTO ME.'

---

* Sung to No. 448, Hymns A. and M.

*No. VII.
The Canopy of Heaven.

THE canopy of Heaven,
    Why stretches forth its span
O'er earth's expanse, why lasts it
    Since first its years began?
Not solely for His pleasure
    Who framed the world so fair,
But men to cheer and gladden
    All things created were.
    To celebrate His goodness
        Your art and skill employ,
    "Who giveth all things richly
        For all men to enjoy."

Why pencils He the flowers
    With wondrous grace and art?
Or why to tender blossoms
    Should He sweet scent impart?
Or to the feathered songsters,
    Why teaches He their strain?
Why spreads He varied verdure
    O'er hill, and dale, and plain?
    To celebrate, &c.

With countless blooms why decks He
    The ever-welcome Spring?
Or Summer still and Autumn,
    Their stores why bids He bring?
For men the seasons ever,
    Throughout the changing year,
Come laden with fresh blessings,
    And in due course appear.
    To celebrate, &c. Amen.

* Music by Berthold Tours.

Harvest Hymns.

No. 1.
Processional Harvest Hymn.

"God is the King of all the earth, sing ye praises with understanding."

REJOICE in your GOD, all ye people of earth,
    O enter His Courts with a song;
Be glad in His presence with Heaven-taught
    mirth,
    The while ye His praises prolong:
As dutiful liegemen draw near to your LORD,
    To render the homage of love;
In trustful reliance on that mighty Word
    That ruleth below and above.

The King of all kings and the FATHER of all
    Is He, whose dependents are ye;
He gladdens His people, He waits for their call,
    And fain their allegiance would see.
That ye are His subjects ye come to proclaim,
    His soldiers yourselves to profess,
To do Him obeisance, to honour His Name,
    Your faith before men to confess.

Be grateful to Him for the fruits of the field,
    To Him your thank-offerings bring;
Your soul's best affections devotedly yield,
    Whilst of His sure mercies ye sing.
With hearts, lips, and lives the CREATOR adore,
    To you His best gifts He hath given,
He filleth with plenty your basket and store,
    He cheereth with bright hopes of Heaven.

O come, let us offer the incense of prayer,
    From the heart let its odour ascend,
With fervour of love your oblation prepare
    In blessings again to descend:
With hearty accordance then let there be sung
    All glory, and honour, and praise,
To GOD in three Persons by every tongue,
    Our FATHER the Ancient of days. Amen.

* No. II.

Faithful in Thy Love.

"The Lord is good to all: and His tender mercies are over all His works."

FAITHFUL in Thy love
    As the seasons move,
A FATHER'S hand, in Thine, O GOD, we hail:
    Still as ages run
    Thy behest is done,
The seed-time and the Harvest do not fail.

    Who, but Thou, doth dress
    In their loveliness
All hills and smiling vales with verdant sheen?
    Thou in dewy meed
    Flocks and herds dost feed:
'Tis Thou Who spreadest out their pasture green.

---

* Tune composed for this Hymn by J. B. Dykes, Mus. Doc.

Who, but Thou, the flowers
In the summer hours
Doth paint and pencil with a skill Divine?
They with incense sweet
Their CREATOR greet;
The joy of these is ours, the glory Thine.

Who, but Thou, the rills
Sparkling 'mid the hills
Doth fill with former and with latter rain?
Who, but Thou, with dew
Nature doth renew,
And cause the blade to spring, and swell the grain?

Thou, with vest of gold,
Dost the earth enfold,
Bedecking yearly thus her fruitful breast:
Thus to all their food
Giver of all good
Thou givest, and they gather; be Thou blest!

Thee, O TRINITY,
In dread UNITY,
All we, the creatures of Thy hand, do praise:
Thy Creation's song
Join we to prolong,
While our glad hymns of glory we upraise. Alleluia.
Amen.

No. III.

Put on thy Strength, O Zion.

"Be joyful, O earth: break forth into singing, O mountains."

PUT on thy strength, O Zion,
   Awake, rejoice, and sing;
   To praise thy GOD and FATHER
   Thy yearly tribute bring.
      Break forth once more, O Zion,
      In strains of thankful song,
      Let notes of joy and gladness
      Be heard Thy Courts among.

Our GOD, Who all things giveth
  And o'er the earth doth reign,
In Whom each creature liveth,
  We magnify again.
    Break forth, &c.

We praise Him Who reserveth
  The harvest weeks to earth,
We bless Him Who preserveth
  His people's souls from dearth.
    Break forth, &c.

O Author of salvation,
  Whate'er in life betide,
As wheat Thy people gather
  At Thy last Harvest-tide;
    Then shall Thy Church triumphant
    Upraise th' eternal song,
    And on through countless ages
    Thy praises shall prolong. Amen.

*No. IV.

Gracious God, another Harvest.

"Thou openest Thine hand and fillest all living things with plenteousness."

GRACIOUS God, another Harvest
   By Thy mercy spared to see,
Now we come our glad thanksgivings
   In Thine house to offer Thee;
Whilst in humble adoration
   We Thy Holy Name do bless,
Heav'nly FATHER, we entreat Thee,
   Pardon our unworthiness.

Thou, O GOD, our corn preparest,
   Thou providest for the earth;
Though we plant, Thine is the increase,
   Thou dost save our souls from dearth:
Rich and poor alike depending
   For their life and breath on Thee,
Old and young we come confessing
   Thine exhaustless charity.

On Thee eyes of all have waited
   For the sunshine and the rain,
Now our garners by Thy mercy
   Are replenished once again;
When Thou givest, then we gather—
   Thou dost open wide Thine hand,
With rich stores of plenty filling
   Far and wide our favour'd land.

---

* Music by J. Langran.

From Thee come good gifts and perfect;
  Gifts of Providence and grace,
Needful for the soul and body,
  To Thy bounteous hand we trace;
Unto Thee, Almighty FATHER,
  SON, and SPIRIT, glory be :
Alleluia, Alleluia,
  Alleluia unto Thee. Amen.

No. V.

To Thee, Who art the Harvest's Lord.

" Ye shall bring a sheaf of the first-fruits of your harvest unto the priest, and he shall wave the sheaf before the Lord to be accepted for you."

O Thee, Who art the Harvest's LORD,
  In olden days they brought
The sheaf of first-fruits at Thy word,
  And thus Thy favour sought.

Thine Israel then Thou didst command
  Thy power and love to own,
In spreading plenty o'er their land,
  And blessing seed-corn sown.

Now we, as they, our tribute bring
  To this, Thy house of prayer,
And whilst of Harvest gifts we sing,
  We crave Thy blessing there.

We render homage unto Thee,
  Our great High Priest and Head,
Who didst vouchsafe for us to be
  " The first-fruits of the dead."

When from the furrows of the grave
  Earth shall its full ears yield,
May we amid the wheat-corn wave
  In that last Harvest field. Amen.

* No. VI.

From the Priceless Harvest.

"Let us come before His presence with thanksgiving."

FROM the priceless harvest
  With its golden yield,
From the stores in-gathered
  Of each fruitful field,
From the countless tokens
  Of our FATHER's love;
Onward to His Temple
  Choirs and people move.
    Our glad song upraising,
      Once again we come,
    GOD our FATHER praising,
      At our Harvest home.

---

* Music by Dean Alford.

For the blade of promise
  In the early year,
For the wondrous increase
  Of the full ripe ear;
For the rain and sunshine
  Sent to bless the land,
For the vast outpouring
  From His bounteous hand.
    Our glad song, &c.

For the dew He sendeth
  On our earth-worn hearts,
For the warmth so genial
  Grace Divine imparts,
Breathings of His SPIRIT,
  Quick'ning souls to life;
For the aid He giveth
  In the daily strife.
    Our glad song, &c.

For that greater Harvest
  Of immortal souls,
Ever being garner'd
  As time onward rolls.
Hither come and bless Him,
  Earth and Heaven's King;
Hither your thank-off'rings
  For His mercies bring.
    Our glad song, &c.

No. VII.
With Thankful Heart, with Tuneful Voice.

" And the multitudes cried Hosanna!"

WITH thankful heart, with tuneful voice,
Whilst we in our good LORD rejoice,
  Sing we loud Hosannas!
As in thanksgiving notes we raise
The yearly tribute of our praise,
  Sing we loud Hosannas!

To GOD, Who doth His flock sustain,
Who hath matured the golden grain,
  Sing we loud Hosannas!
To Him Who doth His promise still
In mercy and in love fulfil,
  Sing we loud Hosannas!

To CHRIST, the first-fruits of the dead,
Pledge of that Harvest—our great Head,
  Sing we loud Hosannas!
Who still His ransomed gathers in
Victorious over death and sin,
  Sing we loud Hosannas!

To GOD the SPIRIT, by Whose grace
Good gifts are lavished on our race,
  Sing we loud Hosannas!
To co-eternal TRINITY
In ever-blessed UNITY,
  Hosanna in the highest! Amen.

*No. VIII.

The Harvest-tide Oblation.

" Whoso offereth Me thanks and praise he honoureth Me."

ONCE more the sheaves are gathered,
 Once more the garner's stored,
Thy promise faithful ever,
 Be Thy great Name adored.
  Our Harvest-tide oblation,
   Each year, O GOD, we bring;
  To Thee be praise and glory,
   Our FATHER, LORD, and KING.

The eyes of all Thy creatures
 Have waited once again
On Thee, Who ever sendest
 The sunshine and the rain.
  Our Harvest-tide, &c.

Their skill and toil together
 Men fail not to combine,
But "Thou their corn preparest,"
 The increase all is Thine.
  Our Harvest-tide, &c.

While for Thy constant mercies
 Our lips do sing Thy praise,
Our souls to Heavenly blessings
 We pray Thee, LORD, to raise.
  Our Harvest-tide, &c.

---

* Music from the Lausanne Psalter.

Of souls the priceless harvest
    Thou, GOD, alone canst bless:
Send many forth to labour,
    And crown them with success.
        Our Harvest-tide, &c.

And when the angel reapers
    Shall gather in Thy store,
Then may we in Thy garner
    Be safe for evermore.
        Our Harvest-tide, &c. Amen.

* No. IX.

The Harvest=tide Thanksgiving.

"*They joy before Thee, according to the joy in Harvest.*"

REAT Giver of all good, to Thee again
    We humbly now present, in joyous strain,
        Our Harvest-tide Thanksgiving.

To Thee, in Whom we live and move, we come
To praise Thee for the sheaves brought safely home,
    With Harvest-tide Thanksgiving.

Thou dost prepare our corn—and year by year
Before Thine altar, LORD, will we appear
    With Harvest-tide Thanksgiving.

---

* Set to music by Sir Jos. Barnby, A.D. 1863. Published in "The Musical Times"; also in "The Hymnary," "The Irish Church Hymnal," "The Book of Praise," "The Wesleyan Sunday School Hymnal," "The S.P.C.K. Supplement," etc.

Thine was the former and the latter rain,
Enriching earth, and calling forth again
   The Harvest-tide Thanksgiving.

Thou openest wide, great GOD, Thy bounteous hand,
And far and wide ascends from all the land
   Glad Harvest-tide Thanksgiving.

Thou fillest all that live with plenteousness;
They, in return, Thy sacred Name should bless
   In Harvest-tide Thanksgiving.

Thy clouds drop fatness on the teeming earth;
Accept these festal songs of "reverent mirth,"
   This Harvest-tide Thanksgiving.

The year is crowned with goodness, LORD, by Thee;
Then meet it is that aye should offered be
   The Harvest-tide Thanksgiving.

On every side the little hills rejoice,
On every side sounds forth the grateful voice
   Of Harvest-tide Thanksgiving.

The valleys, thick with corn, do laugh and sing,
Let all, who sow and reap, together bring
   Their Harvest-tide Thanksgiving.

For all the blessings, LORD, Thy mercy gave,
Praise we with this best member that we have,
   In Harvest-tide Thanksgiving.

To Thee, O TRINITY in UNITY,
All glory, laud, and endless homage be
   In Harvest-tide Thanksgiving. Amen.

Hymns for Holy Matrimony.

See Litany on page 134, to be sung while awaiting the Bride.

* No. I.

Processional Hymn.

WHEN MEETING THE BRIDAL PARTY AT THE CHURCH DOOR.

TO the presence chamber
   Of our LORD and KING,
  We, His waiting people,
   Hither come to bring
Compact to be sealèd
  In His Name to-day.
Troth here to be plighted,
  To abide alway.

Hither come we seeking
  Him to be our Guest:
Joys are yet more joyous
  By our Master blest.
He, the meek and lowly,
  Deigns, when sought, to come,
Hearts to cheer and gladden
  In our earthly home.

---

* From a musical setting of the Marriage Service, music by Rev. Canon F. A. J. Hervey, Chaplain in Ordinary to the Queen, and H.R.H. the Prince of Wales.

HYMNS FOR HOLY MATRIMONY.

Jesu, Lord, we pray Thee,
  These espousals grace;
Shed on these Thy servants
  Brightness of Thy face.
Through this life so changeful,
  Thou, Who changest not,
Ever be their portion,
  And maintain their lot.*

From Thee, Gracious Father,
  Blessings ever flow,
Through Thee, Heavenly Bridegroom,
  For Thy Spouse below.
Holy Ghost, proceeding
  From the Sire and Son,
Lead and guide Thy servants
  Till their days be done. Amen.

No. II.

Processional Hymn.

The Choir, when not Meeting the Bridal Party at the Church Door, may sing, as the Bride advances to the Chancel Step,

WITH joyous festal strain
  Thy sacred Courts, O Lord, we tread to-day,
Be with this Bridal Train,
  They for Thy holy Presence come to pray.

---

* " The Lord Himself is the portion of mine inheritance, and of my cup: Thou shalt maintain my lot."—*Psalm xvi.* 6.

As onward now we move,
Before Thine Altar, gracious Lord, to kneel,
  O fill our hearts with love
To Thee, and Thine own love to us reveal.

Our joys O sanctify,
Begun, continued, ended, Lord, in Thee,
  'Tis Thine to beautify
And not disdain this our festivity.

Else, fleeting joys of earth
Unsanctified, must in confusion end:
  Else, mortals' short-lived mirth
By Thee unblest, shall soon with sorrow blend.

Then in Thy faith and fear,
Encouraged, Father, by Thy love we come,
  And humbly now draw near
To crave Thy blessing on the Bride's new home.
                                            Amen.

No. III.

Final Hymn.

MAY BE SUNG KNEELING, BEFORE THE BRIDAL PARTY RETIRE,
OR AS A RETROCESSIONAL HYMN.

JESU, Lord, Thy holy Presence
    Once at Cana gladness brought,
  When the marriage tie to honour,
    Thy first miracle was wrought.
Still Thy Church is claiming Thee,
Gracious wedding Guest to be.

With Thy Spouse a mystic union,
  Thine it was to consecrate;
Here her newly-wedded members
  "For Thy loving-kindness wait,"*
Gifts and graces from on high,
Heart and life to sanctify.

On Thy servant, on Thy handmaid,
  Who before Thine altar kneel,
Seeking at Thy hands a blessing,
  As their sacred vow they seal,
Ever Thy best gifts bestow,
As through life they onward go.

May they to the solemn compact
  Of their wedlock faithful prove,
In their LORD's own Name united
  By the bonds of changeless love,
Thine, their life-long union o'er,
May they be for evermore. Amen.

---

* "We wait for Thy loving-kindness, O God, in the midst of Thy temple."—*Psalm xlviii.* 8.

Litanies for Church Seasons.

*No. I.—ADVENT.
Litany of the Four Comings.

(1) "*They found the Babe, lying in a manger.*"
(2) "*And when He was come into Jerusalem all the city was moved.*"
(3) "*If I will that he tarry till I come, what is that to thee?*"
(4) "*Behold, He cometh with clouds, and every eye shall see Him.*"

(1) JESU, our opening year
    Once more proclaims Thee near,
Thy waiting people turn again to Thee;
By Thy first Advent in humility,
    O SAVIOUR, we beseech Thee, hear us.

(2) While now Hosannas ring,
    Thou comest as a King
In lowly guise, and yet in regal state—
By that dread pomp that shall upon Thee wait,
    O SAVIOUR, we beseech Thee, hear us.

(3) Again we see Thee come
    Jerusalem to doom,
Type of the terrors of the last great day:
By those stern judgments Thou didst then display,
    O SAVIOUR, we beseech Thee, hear us.

(4) When every eye shall see
    Thine awful Majesty,
By that last Advent, grant us to abide
Amid Thy chosen gathered at Thy side;
    O SAVIOUR, we beseech Thee, hear us.

---

* From "Advent-tide," a Service of Sacred Song. Set to music by A. H. Brown.

*No. II.—CHRISTMAS.

Litany of the Nativity.

HOLY JESU, Heavenly King,
By the love that did Thee bring
For a lost world's ransoming—
Hear us, Blest EMMANUEL!

For the pity Thou didst feel
For man's wounds Thou wouldest heal,
Turning woe to endless weal—
Hear us, blest EMMANUEL!

By that first sweet Christmas song
Ages echo all along,
Chanted by the angel throng—
Hear us, Blest EMMANUEL!

By Thy wondrous lowly Birth
Gladd'ning all the sons of earth,
As they sing its priceless worth—
Hear us, Blest EMMANUEL!

By the deep humility
Of Thine helpless Infancy,
Deigning Child of earth to be—
Hear us, Blest EMMANUEL!

By the mercy, grace, and love
Prompting Thee for us to move
From the realms of bliss above—
Hear us, Blest EMMANUEL!

---

* From "Christmas-tide," a Service of Sacred Song. Set to music by A. H. Brown.

No. III.

Litany of the Epiphany.

FOUNDED ON THE SCRIPTURES FOR EPIPHANY-TIDE.

 THOU, Who didst the Eastern sages call,
By wondrous star, unto Thy Manger-throne,
Sign of the breach in that " Partition wall "
(Ep.) That stood 'twixt Gentile nations and Thine Own,
By Thine Epiphany, LORD JESU, hear us.

*(1) Made manifest in early childhood's days
Amid the Doctors : or, at Cana's feast,
(2) When water, turned to wine, Thy might displays;
(3) Or, when from sickness Thou dost grant release,
By Thine Epiphany, LORD JESU, hear us.

(4) Or when the winds and waves Thy Word obey,
Or demons, trembling, wail at Thy command,
(5) Or Thou Thyself dost shadow forth the Day
When as the wheat or tares all flesh shall stand,
By that Epiphany, LORD JESU, hear us.

(6) When at that Day Thou shalt be manifest,
Borne on the clouds in awful Majesty,
By tribes of earth and angel hosts confest,
Then, in Thy Kingdom, grant us place with Thee;
In that Epiphany, LORD JESU, save us. Amen.

---

* The figures refer to the Gospels for the Sundays after the Epiphany.

LITANIES FOR CHURCH SEASONS.

*No. IV.—GOOD FRIDAY.
Litany of the Seven Last Words.

"Charity never faileth."

JESU, Thou art aye the same,
 From Thy bitter cross of shame
 Words of love Thou dost proclaim—
  LAMB OF GOD, REDEEMER.

(1) "FATHER, forgive them, for they know not what they do."—*S. Luke xxiii.* 34.

 While upon th' accursèd tree
 Ruthless hands are nailing Thee,
 That they may forgiven be,
  LAMB OF GOD, Thou prayest.

(2) "Verily I say unto Thee, To-day shalt Thou be with Me in Paradise."—*S. Luke xxiii.* 43.

 At the malefactor's cries,
 Promise sure of Paradise,
 First-fruits of Thy sacrifice.
  LAMB OF GOD, Thou givest.

(3) "Woman, behold thy Son: then saith He to the disciple, Behold thy mother."—*S. John xix.* 27.

 Well Thy gentle words declare
 How belov'd Thy chosen are—
 For Thy mother tender care
  LAMB OF GOD, Thou shewest.

---

* From "Passion-tide," a Service of Sacred Song. Set to music by A. H. Brown.

(4) "ELI, ELI, lama Sabacthani—My GOD, My GOD, why hast Thou forsaken Me?"—*S. Matt. xxvii.* 46.

> Loudly 'neath that darken'd sky,
> Once again we hear Thee cry,
> In Thy lonesome agony,
>> LAMB OF GOD, forsaken.

(5) "I thirst."—*S. John xix.* 28.

> Pain must needs have done its worst
> When from those parch'd lips there burst
> Those dire words of awe, "I thirst,"
>> LAMB OF GOD, o'erwhelmèd.

(6) "It is finished."—*S. John xix.* 30.

> It is finished! "Bruis'd Thine heel!" *
> Woe endur'd for lasting weal,
> Wounds—the scars of sin to heal,
>> LAMB OF GOD, the Victim!

(7) "FATHER, into Thy hands I commend My spirit."
S. Luke xxiii. 46.

> Ere Thy thorn-crown'd head shall bow,
> Thine immortal Spirit now
> To Thy FATHER's keeping Thou,
>> LAMB OF GOD commendest.

---

* Genesis iii. 15.

☦

*No. V.—EASTER.

Litany of the Resurrection.

JESU, Who didst pass once more to life †
    From out the gloomy grave and gate of death;
O'er sin and Satan, Victor in the strife,
    In human flesh again to breathe man's breath—
        We pray Thee, by Thy Resurrection power,
        Good LORD, deliver us.

That print of nails—that spear-mark in Thy side
    Thou barest that the doubting may believe:
While these our falt'ring faith still seem to chide,
    And we, through want of trust, Thy SPIRIT grieve,
        We pray Thee, &c.

Thou, Who dost hold the keys of death and hell,
    Thine earthly mission closed, Thy conflict o'er—
Hear us, as we in strains of triumph tell
    How Thou didst rise to live for evermore.
        We pray Thee, &c.

Baptized into Thy death, henceforth to live
    By Thee a life of Faith and Hope and Love,
Ever anew to us Thy succour give,
    And our affections raise to things above.
        We pray Thee, &c.

---

* Music by A. H. Brown.

† "Man He rose, since Man He died: the Manhood quickened but the GODHEAD Quickener. Man, then, as touching the Flesh, GOD, now over all things: for now we know CHRIST no longer after the flesh, but we owe it to the flesh that we know Him, as become the First-fruits of them that slept and the First-Begotten of the dead."—*S. Ambrose.*

*No. VI.
Litany of the Ascension.

JESU, Lord, ascended
   Now within the veil,
Whither Thou didst enter,
   Where Thou dost prevail;
Thou our great Forerunner,
   Thither gone to plead,
With our Heavenly FATHER
   There to intercede—
CHRIST, we pray Thee, hear us!

By th' eternal glory
   Thou didst lay aside,
From the Highest coming,
   Deigning to abide
In that humble dwelling
   'Mid the sons of earth—
Raising thus the fallen
   By Thy lowly birth.
CHRIST, we pray Thee, hear us!

By Thine exaltation
   To the realms of light,
Unto bliss returning—
   To those mansions bright;
Of Thy people mindful
   Thou wilt ever be,
Never now rejecting
   Those who come to Thee—
CHRIST, we pray Thee, hear us!

---

* From "Ascension-tide," a Service of Sacred Song. Set to music by Rev. Canon F. A. J. Hervey, Chaplain to H.R.H. the Prince of Wales.

By that last dread advent,
On the clouds again,
At Thy seat of judgment
All men to arraign;
Grant us then to enter
Heaven's gates within,
By Thy blood redeemèd,
Cleansèd from our sin:
CHRIST, we pray Thee, hear us.

No. VII.

Litany for Whitsuntide.

HOLY GHOST, Who in primeval day,
When earth was formless and yet darkness reigned,
Didst, in Creation, quickening power display,
Hear us, Life-giving PARACLETE.

O LORD of power, O Breath of Heavenly life,
By Whom man first "became a living soul,"
And still all nature with that Breath is rife,
Revive us, Holy COMFORTER.

On Thine inheritance a gracious rain
Outpour, of Thy refreshment great our need!
O give us comfort of Thy help again,
With Thy free Spirit stablish us.

No. VIII.

Litany of the Holy Trinity.

"And one cried unto another and said, Holy, Holy, Holy is the Lord of Hosts."

HOLY, Blessed TRINITY,
   Three in One and One in Three,
   Dread, mysterious UNITY,
     Bless, preserve, and keep us.
With the heart we would believe,
And from Thee more faith receive,
Praying ere Thine House we leave,
    Bless, preserve, and keep us.

If the tempter should betray,
If we err and go astray,
And forsake the narrow way,
   Holy FATHER, pardon.
Make Thy word within us burn,
So to Thee we shall return,
Thou the contrite wilt not spurn,
   Holy FATHER, pardon.

JESU, Who for us didst bleed,
And dost live to intercede,
Help us in our time of need,
   Holy SON, O plead Thou.
In our clouded, darksome days,
'Mid the error of our ways,
Cheer Thou us with Thy bright rays,
   Holy SPIRIT, lead Thou.

As through life we onward move
Teach us more Thine House to love,
Leading to Thy Courts above,
  Now, henceforth and ever.
Grant us grateful hearts to bring
While we Alleluias sing
To our SAVIOUR, LORD, and KING,
  Now, henceforth and ever. Amen.

* No. IX.

Children's Litany to the Holy Trinity.

ATHER, from Thy Throne on high,
Listen to our humble cry,
Hear our solemn Litany—
    We beseech Thee, hear us.

JESU, blest Redeemer, hear
Us Thy children who draw near,
Asking faith and holy fear—
    We beseech Thee, hear us.

Gracious SPIRIT, heavenly Dove,
Coming ever from above,
Fill us with Thy "fire of love"—
    We beseech Thee, hear us.

Holy, Blessèd, Glorious Three,
In the mystic Unity,
Hear us when we cry to Thee—
    We beseech Thee, hear us.

---

* From a Service for Children, published by Pitman. Music by Canon F. A. J. Hervey, Sandringham.

When with words of praise and prayer
To Thy temple we repair,
Make us glad and joyful there—
    We beseech Thee, hear us.

When within Thy holy place
We, Thy children, seek Thy face,
Fill us with Thy heavenly grace—
    We beseech Thee, hear us.

FATHER, we Thy promise claim,
As of old, so now the same,
When we ask in JESU'S Name—
    We beseech Thee, hear us.

Wayward from Thy paths we stray,
Prone to wander far away,
Yet forsake us not, we pray—
    We beseech Thee, hear us.

Gentle JESU, SAVIOUR meek,
Thou the lost didst come to seek,
Strengthen us—the frail, the weak—
    We beseech Thee, hear us.

Guard and guide us, we implore,
And when this short life is o'er,
Make us Thine for evermore—
    We beseech Thee, hear us.

✠

No. X.
Litany for a Dedication Festival.

THOU, Who, sojourning awhile below
    Amid the dwellings of the sons of men,
Didst not disdain around their Feast to throw
    A halo of Thy Holy Presence then,
        Be present at our Dedication Festival.

Thou didst unhallow'd traffickers expel
    From sacred precincts of the Temple's shrine—
Thy FATHER'S House, wherein He fain would dwell;
    To us Thy suppliants Thine ear incline,
        And sanctify our Dedication Festival.

O grant us somewhat of Thy burning zeal
    To hallow ever this Thine House of Prayer :
O JESU, now Thy grace and love reveal
    To lowly souls, who bow before Thee there,
        And bless us in our Dedication Festival.

No. XI.
Harvest Litany.

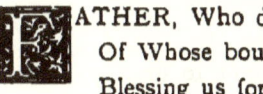ATHER, Who didst all things make,
    Of Whose bounties all partake ;
    Blessing us for JESU'S sake,
        Thee we pray to hear us.

SON, by Whose creative word
    Worlds were made, Who art adored
    As the golden Harvest's LORD,
        Thee we pray to hear us.

HOLY GHOST, Who erst didst brood
O'er the face of chaos rude,
Ere all things were callèd good,
    Thee we pray to hear us.

Blessed TRINITY, once more,
Now the Harvest-weeks are o'er,
For Thy promised yearly store
    We, Thy people, praise Thee.

* No. XII.

A Litany for Holy Matrimony.

SUGGESTED TO BE SUNG, IF TIME ADMIT, WHILE AWAITING THE ARRIVAL OF THE BRIDE AND BRIDEGROOM.

RACIOUS FATHER, GOD of love,
    JESU CHRIST, and Heavenly Dove,
From Thy dwelling-place above,
    In Thy mercy hear us.

Ever blessèd TRINITY,
In our joy and grief to Thee
We and all Thy people flee.
    THREE in ONE, O hear us.

For Thy servant we to-day
And Thy handmaid come to pray:
Grant them grace "through life's rough way."
    Gracious LORD, O hear us.

---

* From a musical setting of the Marriage Service. Music by Rev. Canon Hervey, Domestic Chaplain to H.R.H. the Prince of Wales.

Sanctify the life-long vow
To be sealed before Thee now,
As they in Thy presence bow.
    Holy FATHER, hear us.

Thou Who wedlock's sacred tie
Didst adorn and beautify
With Thy presence,—be Thou nigh,
    Holy JESU, hear us.

O'er life's journey hovering
Fold them 'neath Thy silver wing,
And safe home Thy servants bring.
    HOLY SPIRIT, hear us.

Gracious FATHER, GOD of love,
JESU CHRIST, and Heavenly DOVE,
From Thy dwelling-place above,
    THREE in ONE, O hear us. Amen.

OCCASIONAL HYMNS.

*Hymn for the Dedication of an Organ.

WHEN the morning stars together
   Their primeval anthem sang,
When outstretched by Thee, CREATOR,
   Yon bright vault of Heaven rang
With glad shouts of acclamation,
   Raised by "Sons of GOD" to Thee;
Thine it was to give them being,
   Theirs, celestial choir to be.

By Thy will, as when created,
   Still o'erhangs the spangled sky,
Earth and vast expanse of ocean,
   Thee, their Maker, glorify:
While from angels and archangels
   Still pours forth the ceaseless strain,
Multitudes with myriad voices,
   Echoing on the glad refrain.

---

* Sung at the Dedication of the New Organ in Exeter Cathedral, A.D. 1891. Sung also, both at Matins and Evensong, at the Festival in Peterborough Cathedral, at the Dedication of the New Organ, May 10th, A.D. 1894. Music by Rev. A. W. Hamilton-Gell, Mus. Bac.

Unto Thee, Who in all ages
   Wisdom gavest at Thy will,
Unto Thee, Who aye inspirest
   Sons of men in craft and skill,
We, in humble adoration
   Of Thine awful Majesty,
Come, to-day, this work completed
   Here to dedicate to Thee.

Thine the meed of Alleluias:
   Unto Thee Thy people raise
For all works begun and ended,
   Joyously their strains of praise;
Rising from the stately minster
   Day by day the years along,
Or from fane of lowly hamlet,
   Rolls the tide of sacred song.

Vaulted roofs and cluster'd pillars
   Bear aloft the waves of sound;
Clarions shrill and diapasons
   Sounding forth their tones profound,
In our souls conspire to waken
   Grateful homage due to Thee—
Types of harmony unending,
   In that Temple yet to be.

Lord, vouchsafe Thy heavenly blessing,
   As we consecrate to-day
This our off'ring in Thine honour,
   For Thy service here alway:
Train our souls for Heaven's worship,
   In this Holy House begun,
In the Name and for the merits
   Of Thy dear and only Son. Amen.

Hymn for the Baptism of an Adult.

"Thus it becometh us to fulfil all righteousness."

LORD, Who didst for us in Jordan
  In Baptismal waters stand,
Needing no such rite, yet willing
  To fulfil Thine own command:
Bless Thy suppliant servant now
Pledging here his solemn vow.

Then the pure and blessèd SPIRIT
  Hover'd o'er Thee as a Dove,
When the FATHER'S voice proclaim'd Thee
  SON of His Eternal Love.
With that HOLY SPIRIT now
Seal Thy servant's solemn vow.

Straightway from that holy unction
  To temptation Thou wast led,
Teaching us how snares await us
  In the paths of life we tread:
Strengthen this Thy servant now
Made Thine own by solemn vow.

Thou, Who in Thine early Childhood
  Didst Thy Heavenly FATHER serve,
Thou, Who never in Thy Manhood
  Didst from path of duty swerve,
Succour this Thy servant now,
Give him grace to keep his vow.

Hymns for Temperance Meetings.

*No. I.
Gather, Comrades, Gather.

"Ye shall not go out with haste, nor by flight, for the Lord will go before you, and the God of Israel will be your rereward."
—Isaiah LII. 12.

GATHER, comrades, gather,
   In your ranks to-day,
For the Lord doth need you,
   Hear your Captain say.
Sisters all, we greet you,
   For our cause who feel,
Brothers, here we meet you,
   For the common weal.

We, as trusty liegemen
   Of our Heavenly Lord,
Own one bond of union
   In one glad accord :
One the foe that fronts us,
   One the battle-field ;
One the might that nerves us
   Weapons tried to wield.
      Gather, comrades, &c.

None must halt or waver
   In the constant fray,
Still must our advance be
   Firm in its array.

---

* Sung at the Jubilee of the Rechabites in Exeter and Plymouth.

'Neath the red cross banner,
  Ranged against the foe:
Still the battle rages,
  Forward we must go.
    Gather, comrades, &c.

Be not faint nor weary,
  Brothers, comrades true,
Pledg'd is our alliance
  Deeds of faith to do:
Duty be our watchword,
  Grace our staff and stay,
GOD our cause shall prosper,
  We shall win the day.
    Gather, comrades, &c.

* No. II.

Lord, look down on us, Thy Servants.

"*He bindeth the floods from overflowing.*"—JOB XXVIII. 11.
"*He shall turn away ungodliness from Jacob.*"—ROM. XI. 26.

LORD, look down on us, Thy servants,
  Gather'd in Thy Name to-day,
Our deep need before Thee bringing,
  For Thine aid we humbly pray.
Hear us, Heav'nly FATHER, hear us,
  Grant Thy servants grace to be,
In all righteous efforts striving
  Earnest labourers for Thee.

---

* Sung in Exeter Cathedral at the Jubilee of the Rechabites; also at the Plymouth gathering.   Music by Rev. T. C. Lewis.

Now, for "Thy most gracious favour
  In our doings," LORD, we wait,
Fresh resolves to labour for Thee
  In Thy Name we consecrate;
Knit us closely to each other,
  In one bond of unity,
Grant us for each tempted brother
  Tender-hearted sympathy.

Look upon our land that mourneth
  In its shame and sore distress;
"Bind the floods from overflowing,"
  "Turn away ungodliness."
What, if swell the mighty waters
  Raging ever horribly,
Mightier Thou—the LORD JEHOVAH—
  Ruling on Thy Throne on high.

We the clay, and Thou the Potter,
  Fit and frame us, LORD, to be
"Vessels unto honour" garnish'd
  For Thine House eternally;
Lips and lives all glory giving
  To the FATHER and the SON,
With the HOLY SPIRIT, ever
  While the ages yet shall run. Amen.

*Hymn for those who Travel by Land or Water.

"Safety is of the Lord."

LORD, most holy, God most mighty,
   Let our cry come unto Thee:
Save from perils all who journey
   O'er the land, and on the sea,
'Neath the shadow of Thy wing
All our dear ones sheltering.

Thou, Who didst sustain Thy people
   As they wandered in the wild,
Shielding them from instant danger
   Or when crafty foe beguiled,
Still protect Thine Israël;
Thou their Keeper, all is well.

In their going, in their coming,
   At all times, in every place,
From all hurt to soul and body
   As they run their earthly race,
GUARDIAN, Who dost never sleep,
Those we love in safety keep.

Pilgrims, sojourners, and strangers,
   We, as all our fathers were,
Having no abiding city,
   To Jerusalem repair;
Bring us—all life's journeys o'er,
There to dwell for evermore.

---

* Written by request, for the "Home Hymn Book." Adapted to an ancient melody.

Hymn for the Dedication of Church Bells.

"*Rejoice with them that do rejoice, and weep with them that weep.*"

  IN the Name of God the FATHER,
   In the Name of God the SON,
   In the Name of God the SPIRIT,
    Holy Blessed Three in One—
  We Thy people come to offer
  Work for this Thy Temple done.

  Like as in the olden ages
   Trumpets did Thy people call,
  Bidding Israël assemble
   In their numbers, one and all;
  So, in such-like sacred office
   We these bells do now install.

  In all times of Joy and Sorrow,
   With their voice of melody,
  Pealing forth their notes of gladness,
   Or in mournful minstrelsy,
  JESU, LORD, they teach Thy lesson
   Unto all,—sweet sympathy.*

---

* "As members of the body of CHRIST, to take part in others' joy, is as much a duty of such membership as to take part in their sorrow."—*Bishop Walsham How.*

FOR THE DEDICATION OF CHURCH BELLS.

This our solemn Dedication,
   Gracious God, accept we pray,
Grant us here Thy Benediction
   In Thy Holy House to-day,
O " prevent us, and our doings
   Further with Thy help alway."

Not to us, O Lord, most mighty,
   Not to us, but unto Thee
Be ascribed the laud and honour
   Unto Thy dread Majesty
Of the fruit of all our labour—
   Praise be Thine eternally.
            Alleluia! Amen.

Hymn for the Opening,
or for the
Re=Dedication of Church Bells.

*Set to an Ancient Hebrew Melody (Hymns A. & M. 601).

"*A Voice from the Temple.*"—Isaiah LXVI. 6.

† *Precentor.* ONG since in by-gone days
    Our fathers unto Thee,
O God, this House of Prayer did raise
    Thine Own to be.

Choir and People. And from its sacred walls,
    With sweet and solemn sound,
They set on high a voice that calls
    On all around.

Solo. A trust from sire to son
    That purpose to fulfil,
Age after age has handed on,
    Abiding still.

People. Ever be ours to stay,
    For ages yet to come,
All progress here of dire decay
    In this,—man's home.

Solo. Here still the tuneful chime
    Its summons shall proclaim,
To lift our souls from things of time—
    To bless Thy Name—

---

* This ancient arrangement for Precentor and People is noted in Dr. Julian's "Dictionary of Hymnology."

† This hymn may, if preferred, be sung full, throughout.

FOR THE OPENING OF CHURCH BELLS.

People. To render thanks and praise—
   To hear Thy Holy Word—
  While earth-worn hearts to Thee we raise,
  Our Gracious LORD.

Solo. For sacred use alone
   These bells designed to be,
  We dedicate anew,—each tone
   Adoringly.
People. On us their constant call
   To serve Thee—GOD of Love,
  Preparing for high Festival
   In Courts above.

Solo. In this Thy House of Prayer
   Grant, Gracious GOD, that we
  May by our words and deeds declare
   Our faith in Thee.
People. And while the ages run,
   From men and Angel-host,
  Be ceaseless praise to FATHER, SON,
   And HOLY GHOST. Amen.

✠

Hymn.

Written by Request, and Sung in Procession at the Benediction of the New School House for Girls, Clewer S. Stephen (Windsor).

RAISE we gladsome voices,
    As to-day we meet,
  Render we thanksgiving
    For this work complete.
Now with hearts elated,
    Schoolmates we are come,
Asking Heavenly Blessing
    On our Childhood's Home.
    Holy, Blessed Jesu,
      Take us by the hand,
    Guide us thro' life's journey
      To the Better Land.

In this place of Training
    Thro' our early life,
Seek we kindly guidance
    Far from harm and strife.
Here the pliant branches
    Of the future tree
With due care are bended
    Into symmetry.
    Holy, &c.

Here our earthly Guardians
    Watch with hopes and fears,
In parental fondness,
    O'er our tender years.

Of the world's temptations
  Give us holy dread,
As, beset with danger,
  We our pathway tread.
    Holy, &c

Jesu, by Thy Childhood
  Spent for us on earth,
Leaving us example
  Of such priceless worth,
Watch in mercy o'er us,
  This our House to bless;
All our doings prosper,
  Crown them with success.
    Holy, &c.

Hymn.

WRITTEN FOR THE UNVEILING OF A MEMORIAL* WINDOW IN THORVERTON CHURCH, A.D. 1889, AND ADAPTED TO BARNBY'S TUNE, "FOR ALL THY SAINTS."†

GOD, Thou didst inspire in ancient days
All workmen's art—Thine Holy House to raise:
Each craftsman still by Thee his skill displays,
    Praise be Thine, to Thee be glory.

Thy Temple to adorn men lavish'd art
In olden time, and we would bear our part,
And off'rings bring with glad and willing heart,
    Praise be Thine, to Thee be glory.

We dedicate to Thee this gift to-day,
Hear us Thy servants as we humbly pray
Thou wilt accept it for Thine House alway,
    Praise be Thine, to Thee be glory.

For good remember him, who for Thy sake
Did freely of his worldly substance take,
That so this House he might more comely make,
    Praise be Thine, to Thee be glory.

We laud Thy Name for those asleep in Thee,
O JESU, grant us grace that they and we
May meet to give Thee thanks eternally.
    Praise be Thine, to Thee be glory.
        Alleluia, Amen.

---

* The gift of E. R. Moxey, Esq., J.P., Cardiff. Unveiled by Rev. Canon Trefusis.

† Sir J. Barnby subsequently sent another tune to the writer for this hymn.

Hymn for Singing on the March

FOR THE CHURCH LADS' BRIGADE.

ADAPTED TO NO. 274, HYMNS ANCIENT AND MODERN.

"LORD of power and might, the Giver
   Of all good," to Thee we sing—
Captain, Thou, of our salvation,
   Our High Priest, Liege-LORD and King.

Rang'd 'neath Thy victorious banner,
   March we onward, sworn to fight
'Gainst the world, the flesh, the devil—
   Trusting in our Master's might.

Lead us on, and we will follow,
   Be at hand to cheer and guide:
Shield us in each dire temptation,
   Lest our faltering footsteps slide.

Shape our childhood by Thy pattern,
   JESU, LORD, our Righteousness,
Make us brave, and true, and loyal,
   Teach us Thine own Manliness.

Soldiers of the Church's army
   Pure in heart must ever be,
Keep before our souls the image
   Of Thy peerless purity.

Meekly Thou didst learn obedience *
To Thy Heavenly FATHER'S will,—
Promptly be it our endeavour
Thy Commandments to fulfil.

So when life's incessant warfare,
And the strife with sin are o'er,
Thou wilt grant Thy faithful liege-men
Rest with Thee for evermore.

---

* " Though He were a Son, yet learned He obedience."—
Hebrews v. 8.

*Hymn for Re-union of former Students, or "Old Boys."

*"We took sweet counsel together:
And walked in the House of God as friends."*

ONCE again in glad re-union
    Hands are clasped and voices blend;
  While our trysting-tide we hallow,
    Prayer and praise to Him ascend,
Who would First-born Brother be
Of the human family.

'Mid earth's scenes, so changeful ever,
    'Mid its dangers manifold,
  O'er us all His eye is watching
    Who each "soul in life doth hold," †
He our FATHER bids us come,
Brothers to His House—our home.

These, the sacred bands that bind us,
    Link the present with the past,
  Friendship's early ties abiding
    Changeless still while life shall last:
Youth's and early manhood's gage,
Firm and true in riper age.

Marching on, our songs uplifted
    No discordant notes shall mar;
  Tokens of that final gath'ring,
    Brothers, these our meetings are.
On that far eternal shore
Partings shall be nevermore.

---

* Written by request of the Head Master for the Devon County School, West Buckland.   † Psalm lxvi. 7, 8, 9.

Hymn for the Girls' Friendly Society.*

"Know ye not that to whom ye yield yourselves servants to obey, his servants ye are to whom ye obey?"—ROMANS VI. 16.

ESU, gracious LORD and Master,
    Hear us as we sing to Thee,
  "Whom to serve is perfect freedom" †—
    We would each Thine handmaid be.

Great High Priest, Who with the feeling
    Of our deep infirmity
Canst be touched, for Thou in all points
    Hast been tempted, like as we, ‡

Succour us amid temptation,
    And our trials manifold,
Tender Shepherd, guard and guide us, §
    Lest we wander from Thy fold.

As we journey ever onward,
    Toiling, fainting in the wild,
To Thine handmaids O "speak friendly" ‖—
    Each one Thine, each erring child.

---

* Written, at the request of Miss L. A. G. Fursdon, for the Exeter Diocesan Branch of the G.F.S. Set to music by A. W. Hamilton-Gell, M.A., Mus. Bac.

† Second Collect for Peace (Matins).   ‡ Heb. iv. 15.

§ Ezek. xxxiv. 12.

‖ "Therefore, behold I will allure her, and bring her into the wilderness and speak *comfortably* (margin 'friendly') unto her" (Hos. ii. 14).

'Mid the snares of town or city,
  Or where'er our lot be cast,
Treading oft in slippery places,
  Bid Thine angels hold us fast. *

Bind us closely to each other,
  Stay our minds on Heav'n above, †
Fill our hearts with holy comfort,
  Knit together in Thy love.

FATHER, now that ancient promise ‡
  Of Thy SPIRIT we would claim ;
Pour it out on Thine handmaidens,
  For we ask in JESU's Name.

JESU, be our Friend and Brother, §
  So when this brief life is o'er,
Friend with friend shall joy together
  In Thy presence evermore.   Amen.

---

* Heb. i. 14.   † Col. ii. 2.   ‡ Acts ii. 18 : from Joel ii. 29.

§ " There is a friend that sticketh closer than a brother " (Prov. xviii. 24; S. John xv. 14, 15; S. Matt. xii. 50).

Hymns for Missions to the Jews.

WRITTEN TO TUNE 306, HYMNS A. AND M., A.D. 1896.

No. I.

"*Beginning at Jerusalem.*"—S. LUKE XXIV. 47.

JESU, LORD and Master,
    When from out the grave
Thou didst rise victorious,
    Mighty now to save,
Thou didst charge Thy servants
    In those forty days,*
From henceforth the Standard
    Of the Cross to raise.

Thine it was to teach them †
    How, in times of old,
By the SPIRIT guided,
    Prophets did unfold
Things that should hereafter
    All fulfillèd be,
Each one in due season,
    LORD, concerning Thee.

This the glorious Gospel
    They must now proclaim—
On men's true repentance,
    Pardon in Thy Name.
This the Church's Charter
    From her Risen LORD!
Now among all nations
    She must preach the Word.

---

* " Being seen of them forty days" (Acts i. 3).
† *cf.* S. Luke xxiv. 44 to 49.

Yet, before all others
  Must Thy chosen Race
Hear the welcome tidings
  Of abounding Grace.*
Thus, in deep compassion,
  Thou didst send to them
"Witnesses," "beginning
  At Jerusalem."

Thou, Who wouldest all men
  Saving truth should know, †
On Thine ancient people
  Mercy, LORD, bestow.
"To Thy flock O fetch them,"
  Lead them, as of old,
"By the One true Shepherd
  To the one true Fold." Amen.

No. II.

MAY BE SUNG TO TUNES 51, 179, 232, OR 302, HYMNS ANCIENT AND MODERN, A.D. 1896.

"Hear the word of the Lord, O ye Nations, and declare it in the isles afar off, and say—He that scattereth Israel will gather him, and keep him, as a shepherd doth his flock. For the Lord hath redeemed Jacob and ransomed him."—JEREMIAH XXXI. 10, 11.

WHEN o'er lands in darkness shrouded
  Thou, the glorious Sun, didst rise,
Chasing gloom and grief and sighing,
  Beaming from the Eastern skies—
Light to Jew and Gentile bringing,
  Giving sight to blinded eyes.

---

* "Where sin abounded, grace did much more abound" (Rom. v. 20).
  † *cf.* Collect for Good Friday.

Then shone forth so great Salvation
   For each kindred tribe and tongue,
Which Thy love had been preparing
   In the ages all along.*
Now to be Thy People's glory,—
   Light, the heathen lands among.

What if Thee the Jews rejected
   In their visitation day,
Still "ungodliness from Jacob"
   Thou didst will "to turn away." †
When, to gather in the outcasts,
   Tender love Thou shalt display.

If, of branches some were broken
   From the ancient parent stem,
Tho' severe amid Thy goodness,
   Mercy is in store for them;
"As a hen her brood doth gather,
   So would'st Thou, Jerusalem."

Haste the day wherein Thine anger
   Thou no longer shalt retain;
Let not, LORD, Thy Death and Passion
   For Thine Israël be vain:
Into their own goodly Olive
   Graff the branches once again. Amen.

---

* S. Luke ii. 29 κ.τ.λ.   † Rom. xi. 26, &c.

Hymn for the Opening of a New School or Class Room.

SUNG AT THE OPENING OF THE NEW CLASS ROOM, THORVERTON, BY ARCHDEACON SANDFORD.

"That our sons may grow up as the young plants : And that our daughters may be as the polished corners of the Temple."
—PSALM CXLIV. 12.

GRACIOUS Lord and Master,
　　Unto Thee, this day,
　We, Thy waiting people,
　　Hither come to pray
For Thy Heavenly blessing
　On our work complete ;
Unto Thee to tender
　Thanks and praises meet.

Thou, the Master Builder,
　Dost bestow on man
For his undertakings
　Wisdom for each plan ; *
Thou, All-wise, inspirest
　Craftsmen with their skill,
Thou dost each enable
　Labours to fulfil.

Hither, for their training,
　Little ones we bring,
Fitting them to serve Thee,
　Their good Lord and King.

---

* "Through wisdom is a house builded : and by understanding it is established" (Prov. xxiv. 3).

Here we fain would guide them,
  Through life's weary way,
To the great Hereafter,
  Ever day by day.

May our "Sons as young plants
  Flourish here and grow;"
Here may all our daughters
  Kindly guidance know:
May Thy grace adorn them,
  So shall they, for Thee,
"As the polished corners
  Of the Temple be."

Grant us to be builded,[*]
  Each one in his place,
"Joints and bands compacted,"[†]
  'Stablish'd by Thy grace.
May we, when life's labours
  Shall at last be o'er,
In the Heavenly mansions
  Serve Thee evermore. Amen.

---

[*] "Ye are God's building" (1 Cor. iii. 9).   [†] Eph. iv. 16.

*Hymns for Missionary Services and Meetings.

No. I.

Give Ear unto our Cry, O Lord.

GIVE ear unto our cry, O LORD,
   While we in deep contrition
Come now before Thee to confess
   Our sins of past omission ;
The failure of our favoured land,
In honouring Thy last command,
   The Church's chief commission.

Wealth and dominion come of Thee ;
   For Thy great ends each nation
With might and power Thou dost endow,
   Of Thee its exaltation !
Thou dost our land to greatness raise,
That men may spread abroad Thy praise,
   And publish Thy salvation.

Arm of the LORD, put on Thy strength,
   The SPIRIT's work reviving ;
Awake, as in the ancient days !
   Bless all who, in Thee striving,
Shall offer alms, and watch and pray,
And bear the burden of the day,
   From Thee fresh grace deriving.

---

* From a Song Service, " The Harvest-Fields of Time," adopted by the S.P.G. Musical Editor, A. H. Brown.

No. II.
As a Beacon o'er the Deep.

AS a beacon o'er the deep
    Fixed with steady light to shine;
As a treasure-house to keep
    Stores for spreading truth divine:
Feebly though our land fulfil,
    Ruler of the world, Thy will,
Grant us all henceforth to be
    Faithful witnesses to Thee.

As a city set on high,
    Seen and known of all around;
JESU, Thee to glorify
    May Thy Church be ever found.
Like the Leaven in the meal,
    Grant that we its members be
Zealous for the wide world's weal,
    Faithful witnesses to Thee.

No. III.
Lo! Plenteous is the Harvest.

SOLO *(Tenor Voice)*.

LO! plenteous is the harvest—
    The labourers are few.

CHORUS.

See far and wide the fields are white,
And alms, and prayers, and toil invite:
To us, benighted heathen lands
Imploring stretch their eager hands.

Solo (*Tenor Voice*).

Lo! plenteous is the harvest—
The labourers are few.

Chorus.

From GOD we freely have received,
But scant the gain for Him achieved;
Redeemed be days that yet remain,
As yet lost ground we may regain.

Solo (*Tenor Voice*).

Lo! plenteous is the harvest—
The labourers are few.

Chorus.

Your hands uplift to GOD on high,
With one united heartfelt cry,
For reapers in the harvest-field,
To gather in the golden yield.

No. IV.
O Lamb of God, for Sinners Slain.

LAMB of GOD, for sinners slain
  To raise earth's fallen sons again
    From darkness to Thy wondrous light!
Thou in Thy love Thy Church hast taught,
All souls to Thee Thou wouldst have brought,
  Since all are precious in Thy sight:
Forth in Thy Name the workmen go,
From Thee they bear the seed they sow:
  The very seed itself Thou art,
Thou their support in all their toil;
Thine to make meet each varied soil—
  "The preparations of the heart."

Thine that exceeding great reward
Thou dost to faithful souls accord,
   Inspired by Thee with love divine :
With joy untold those Thou shalt bless,
Who others turn to righteousness,
   They shall like stars in glory shine :
And from each nation, people, tongue,
Shall rise the never-ending song,
   To Him that sitteth on the throne,
By each one on his harp of gold
The story of the Cross be told,
   And how Thou didst for all atone.

No. V.

The Harvest=Fields of Time.

"LIFT up your eyes and look upon the fields,"
   Their vast expanse a golden promise yields—
      The Harvest-fields of Time.
Amid the murmur of their deep unrest
They call from North and South, from East and West,
      The Harvest-fields of Time.

Lo, now we come, depending on Thy word,
Thee to entreat, Who art the Harvest's LORD,
      For Harvest-fields of Time :
For "not by might, but in Thy SPIRIT's power"
Men toil, while lasts as yet life's little hour,
      In Harvest-fields of Time.

While yet Thy Church no vast ingatherings boasts ;
"O wilt not Thou go forth among her hosts,"
      To Harvest-fields of Time ?

O stir Thy people's will that there may be
Abundant alms-deeds for Thy work and Thee,
    For Harvest-fields of Time.

Still by those arms outstretched on Calvary
Thou willest all men should be drawn to Thee
    From Harvest-fields of Time:
And by Thy dying love, O LORD, do Thou
With zeal afresh inspire Thy people now
    For Harvest-fields of Time.

Grant us "the Charity that hopeth all;"
Grant faith to hearken to that urgent call
    From Harvest-fields of Time.
O'er all the lands Thy SPIRIT's blessings pour,
Until that Day when shall be found no more—
    The Harvest-fields of Time. Amen, Amen.

Hymns for Passing Events.

Two Hymns were Published in "Memorial Tributes" on Her Majesty's Jubilee, a.d. 1887; also two for the Rechabite Jubilee (see Occasional Hymns).

*No. I.
Thanksgiving Hymn.

"He maketh peace in thy borders, and filleth thee with the finest of the wheat."

WE bless our gracious God to-day,
　With joy we come before Him,
　Who, war's dread scourge for us did stay
We praise Him and adore Him.
With grateful hearts we sing
Of our Almighty King:
For us He maketh peace,
And doth our store increase,
Let all the people praise Him.

Of old He brake the battle bow,
He snapped the spears asunder,
Against His people's vengeful foe
The Highest sent His thunder.
On earth He ruleth still,
None may resist His will:
Fierce men He did restrain,
Restoring peace again,
Let all the people praise Him.

---

* Written after the Crimean War, in time of Harvest. Adapted to Hymn A. & M. 378.

We bless His Name with one accord
Who fruitful seasons sends us,
The Prince of Peace—the Harvest's LORD
He guides, and guards, and tends us,
O may He speed the time,
When men of every clime
Shall swords for plough-shares change,
Nor hostile ranks shall range—
And all the earth shall praise Him. Amen.

No. II.

Hymn for the Day of Thanksgiving after the Battle of Tel-el-Kebir.

Sung to the tune of "The Church's One Foundation," Hymns A. & M. 215.

SANCTIONED BY BISHOP TEMPLE FOR USE IN EXETER DIOCESE.

"*He maketh wars to cease in all the world: He breaketh the bow, and knappeth the spear in sunder, and burneth the chariots in the fire. Be still then, and know that I am God: I will be exalted among the heathen, I will be exalted in the earth. The Lord of hosts is with us, the God of Jacob is our refuge.*"
—PSALM XLVI. 9, 10, 11.

HUSH'D is the din of battle,
    And sheath'd the vengeful sword,
The warrior's costly life-blood
    No longer is out-pour'd:
For He Whose power no creature
    Is able to withstand
Hath clos'd the fray of foemen
    Along El-Kebir's strand.

Of old He brake asunder
  The spear and battle-bow
The chariot and horseman—
  Alike He laid them low:
Of all events the issue
  He over-ruleth still:
The good for aye to prosper
  And bring to nought the ill.

And as of victor's prowess
  Men spread the well-earn'd fame,
With one consent unite we
  To magnify His Name:
Who, 'mid the utmost danger
  With England's hosts hath been,
Who erst from fell assassin
  Hath shielded England's Queen.

Of heartfelt glad thanksgiving
  A nation's tribute bring,
While GOD's ne'er-failing mercies
  To us and ours we sing:
He from her harsh oppressors
  Hath Egypt's soil set free,
Who unto Right and Justice
  Inclineth Victory.

September 20th, A.D. 1880.

No. III.

Hymn.

WRITTEN FOR THE TERCENTENARY CELEBRATION OF THE
VICTORY OVER THE SPANISH ARMADA.

Sung at S. Andrew's Church, Plymouth, A.D. 1888.

"*With us is the Lord our God to help us and to fight our battles.*"
—2 CHRON. XXXII. 8.

GOD, our Nation's Refuge
    Throughout long ages past,
  Sole Source of strength and safety
    While yet earth's ages last,
Thou art the God of battles,
    Thine is all victory,
Of all events the issue
    Must ever come of Thee.

When haughty Spain's Armada,
    With all its mighty host,
Led on by warlike chieftains,
    Bore down on Albion's coast,
Thou didst impart true courage,
    Thou didst inspire with skill
Our loyal-hearted leaders
    Their dangerous post to fill.

Thou with the surging tempest *
    Didst scatter far and wide
The foeman's host of vessels,
    In all its pomp and pride;

---

* "*Afflavit Deus, et dissipavit*," motto on the die struck for the medal to commemorate this event, A.D. 1588.

Thine arm it brought salvation,
  The might of Spain it broke,
Thou England's Church and Nation
  Didst save from foreign yoke.

For this and all Thy mercies
  We praise Thee, LORD, to-day:
That Thou wilt still watch o'er us
  Thy humble servants pray;
And when Thy care and goodness
  We sing with glad acclaim,
We and our children's children
  Will bless Thy glorious Name. Amen.

Hymns for Children's Services

*Hymns for Children's Services.

EDITED BY THE AUTHOR AND ARTHUR H. BROWN.

† No. I.

Morning Hymn.

"In Him we live and move and have our being."

THROUGH dangers of the night,
   Thou hast Thy children brought,
O may it be our chief delight,
   To serve Thee as we ought.

By Thee we live and move,
   By Thee our being have,
Day after day our FATHER'S love
   Sustains the life He gave.

To give us light and heat,
   Thou sendest forth the sun,
So LORD, we pray Thee, guide our feet
   Our daily course to run.

That when the day is done
   And night draws nigh again,
Our FATHER'S smile we may have won,
   For hours not spent in vain.

---

* From a Children's Service Book.
† Music by Rev. Sir F. G. Ouseley, Bart.

* No. II.

Evening Hymn.

"*It is Thou, Lord, only Who makest us to dwell in safety.*"

WHEN sinks the sun in Western skies,
    And daylight slowly fades away,
To Thee our hymns, O FATHER, rise,
    To Thee we come to praise and pray.

O guard us in the silent night,
    O fold us all beneath Thy wing;
For we are ever in Thy sight,
    And closely nnto Thee would cling.

When we lie down to peaceful rest,
    And close our eyes in slumber deep,
As birds within their mother's nest
    Thy little children safely keep.

That so when once again the day
    Shall brightly from the darkness break,
Raised from our beds we gladly may,
    To serve our gracious GOD, awake. Amen.

---

* Set to music by Rev. Sir F. G. Ouseley, Bart. Printed in the "Home Hymn Book."

*No. III.

Lord's Day Morning.

"If thou turn away thy foot from the Sabbath from doing thy pleasure on My holy day, then shalt Thou delight thyself in the Lord."

NOT to seek our selfish pleasure,
    Did our GOD His Sabbaths make,
But that we for heavenly treasure
    Worldly things might then forsake.

In our SAVIOUR'S footsteps walking,
    On His path of duty sent,
Not to-day must we be talking
    Of the world, on trifles bent.

JESU, help Thou us in turning
    From the world our feet away,
JESU, guide Thou us in learning
    How to worship, praise and pray.

Sundays here Thy Word has taught us,
    "Holy of the LORD" should be:
They are glimpses Thou hast brought us
    Of eternal joy to see.

---

*Music by A. H. Brown.

*No. IV.

Lord's Day Evening.

"There remaineth a rest to the people of God."

NOW once more Thy day is closing,
  Day Thou madest, LORD, for man:
Best of days for souls reposing
  From the toil of life's short span.
    Golden hours of calm and peace,
    Types of rest that ne'er shall cease.

Here by faith we see Thee standing
  Blessing all met in Thy Name,
Still we hear Thy word commanding
  Us to hallow now the same
    Sunday hours of calm and peace
    Types of rest that ne'er shall cease.

Ere we turn again to-morrow
  To the cares and toils of earth,
Compass'd round with many a sorrow,
  Drawn aside by short-lived mirth,
    Bless to us Thy day of peace
    Type of rest that ne'er shall cease.

By Thy Sacred days, O make us
  Meet to join Thy saints above,
In the week do not forsake us
  Lest we cast away Thy love.
    Ever be these days of peace
    Types of rest that ne'er shall cease.

---

* Music by Rev. T. H. Matthews.

* No. V.

Public Worship.

"Not forsaking the assembling of ourselves together."

HE angel music of the bells †
    Calls from the holy ground,
Hark! how the joyful cadence swells
    With sweet and tuneful sound.

It bids us haste with willing mind
    To hear of our true Home,
It tells us where true joy to find :
    We come, sweet bells, we come.

And when within Thy Temple door,
    Our minds, O FATHER, guide;
On us Thy Holy SPIRIT pour
    When kneeling side by side.

Let no vain thoughts our hearts beguile
    Within Thy House of Prayer,
Nor foolish words, nor silly smile,
    For Thou, O GOD, art there.

---

* Music by Sir F. G. Ouseley, Bart.
† " Think when the bells do chime
    'Tis angels' music."—*Geo. Herbert.*

* No. VI.

Holy Scripture.

"That we through patience and comfort of the Scriptures might have hope."

BLESSÈD LORD, Who for our learning
   Didst the Holy Scriptures give,
Food for our immortal spirits,
   Bread of Life on which to live,
     Ever may Thy children be
     Guided, taught, and fed by Thee.

Grant that we, these Scriptures loving,
   May be led to read and pray,
Marking well, and then digesting,
   This our heavenly food each day:
     Thus may we Thy children be
     Guided, taught, and fed by Thee.

By Thy Sacred Word, O send us
   Comfort, patience, light and life,
Holding fast, as we embrace it,
   Hope amid the daily strife.
     FATHER, may Thy children be
     Guided, taught, and fed by Thee.

Hope in JESUS is our anchor,
   Hope He gives us by His word,
May our hearts and lives be governed
   By the lessons we have heard.
     Thus may all Thy children be
     Guided, LORD, and fed by Thee.

---

* Music by T. Morley.

*No. VII.

Advent.

THE FOUR COMINGS OF CHRIST.

(1) *"They found the Babe lying in a manger."*
(2) *"And when He was come into Jerusalem all the city was moved."*
(3) *"If I will that he tarry till I come what is that to thee?"*
(4) *"Behold He cometh with clouds, and every eye shall see Him."*

(1) WE sing Thy coming, LORD, to-day,
In wonderful humility,
We know that Thou wilt come again
In dread and glorious majesty.

It cheers Thy little ones to think
That Thou wast once a little Child,
That Thou didst not disdain our flesh,
Though "holy, harmless, undefiled."

(2) We joy to read how when of old,
Thou to Jerusalem didst ride,
Thou their Hosannas didst accept
From children singing at Thy side.

(3) But ah! Thou once again didst come,
And didst Thy terrors then display,
That guilty city to destroy,
Type of the future Judgment Day.

(4) O fix our hearts on things above,
And grant to all Thy children grace,
That walking in Thy fear and love,
We may with joy behold Thy face.

---

* Music by Rev. T. R. Matthews.

*No. VIII.

Last Sunday in the Year,

OR FIRST SUNDAY AFTER CHRISTMAS.

"And now, Lord, what is my hope?—Truly my hope is even in Thee."

HE stream of life rolls on,
  The year is almost gone,
    Its last LORD'S Day is here;
Thou comest, LORD, to see
If on each cultur'd tree
    The signs of fruit appear.

Thy Sacred Name we praise
For all Thy holy days
    Thou didst in mercy give.
Whate'er we left undone
While weeks their course have run
    We pray Thee to forgive.

Our lives Thou sparest still
That we may do Thy will,
    And from our sins may flee:
Throughout life's little day
Be Thou our Shield and Stay,
    O GOD, we trust in Thee.

---

* Music by R. Minton Taylor.

*No. IX.

First Day in the Year,

Or Feast of the Circumcision.

"Though He were a Son, yet learned He obedience by the things which He suffered."

NOW a new year opens,
   Now we newly turn
To the Infant SAVIOUR,
   Lessons fresh to learn.

This the holy lesson
   On the year's first day—
JESUS by obedience
   Teaches to obey.

Of Thy Cross thus early
   Tokens Thou dost give,
By Thy wounds Thou healest,
   By Thy death we live.

Not to suffer only
   JESU didst Thou come,
But to leave us way-marks
   Pointing to our home.

In Thy blessed footsteps
   Ever may we tread,
Safe when keeping near Thee,
   By Thy SPIRIT led.

---

* Set to music by Canon F. J. Hervey, and printed in the "American Church Sunday School Hymnal," and in Mrs. Carey Brock's "Children's Hymnal."

* No. X.

Lent.

"Whosoever doth not bear his cross and come after Me, cannot be My disciple."

NONE are so poor and none so weak
   Who for Thee, Lord, no work can do,
Then help us all our cross to take,
   And thus be Thy disciples true.

And now as we in spirit turn
   To see Thee fasting in the wild,
Thy grace to curb our selfish will
   O give to every little child.

In youthful days O may we learn
   How best against Thy foes to fight
And thus upon us we shall take
   Thine easy yoke, Thy burden light.

From toil and strife we may not shrink
   Nor idly lay our weapons down:
Teach all Thy little ones to think
   What mean those words "No Cross, no Crown."

---

* Music by Rev. T. R. Matthews.

* No. XI.

Easter Day.

"Awake up, my glory—awake lute and harp, I myself will awake right early."

AKE, and with the early day
    Haste to greet the Lord, and say
              Alleluia.

Young and old to-day rejoice
Singing all with one glad voice
          Alleluia.

Unto Thee, the King of Kings,
Each one praise and glory brings
          Alleluia.

Thou hast made our Sundays bright
With the rays of Easter light.
          Alleluia.

Thou for us didst taste of death
Breathing once again our breath,
          Alleluia.

Now Thy pains and sorrows o'er,
Thou dost live to die no more.
          Alleluia.

---

* Music by Rev. Canon F. A. J. Hervey.

* No. XII.

Prayer for Faith.

SUNDAY AFTER EASTER, OR S. THOMAS' DAY.

" Be not faithless but believing."

IN all Thou didst while here on earth
Where for our sakes Thou once hadst birth,
      LORD help us to believe.

In Thy great victory o'er the grave
Our souls from sin and death to save,
      LORD help us to believe.

In Thee, the LAMB OF GOD, Who slain
For us, didst wake and rise again,
      LORD help us to believe.

O raise us from the death of sin
That we, through Thee, our crown may win,
      Thus help us to believe.

The nail-prints now we cannot see
Nor spear-mark where they piercèd Thee,
      Yet help us to believe.

Increase our faith, our hope, our love,
O raise our souls to things above
      And help us to believe.

---

* Music by R. Minton Taylor.

*No. XIII.
Ascension Day.

"When He ascended up on high; He led captivity captive, and gave gifts unto men."

FAR up on high
    To yon blue sky
Thou didst ascend to Heaven again,
    Thy great work done
    The battle won
By deeds of love and cross of pain.

    Yet still for earth
    Where Thou hadst birth
We know, blest SAVIOUR, thou dost care;
    Still Thou dost plead
    In time of need
And bend Thine ear to children's prayer.

    Thy word fulfil
    And help us still,
Who see Thee not—but yet believe;
    Help us to pray,
    And day by day
Our prayers and praises, LORD, receive.

    Grant us Thy grace
    To seek Thy face
That when to judgment Thou shalt come,
    Thou mayest greet
    Thine own made meet
To share the joys of Heaven's bright home.

---

* Music by T. Morley.

* No. XIV.

Whitsun Day.

"*The Comforter—Who is the Holy Ghost.*"

COME Thou blessed Spirit,
   Who in tongues of fire
Didst come down from Heaven
   Mortals to inspire.

Come Thou blessed Spirit
   In our hearts to shine,
Be Thou present with us,
   Teach us truths Divine.

Come Thou blessed Spirit
   From the realms above,
With fresh warmth O cheer us
   Come with power and love.

Come Thou blessed Spirit,
   Holy, Heavenly Balm—
O'er our minds so restless
   Breathe Thy peaceful calm.

---

* Music by A. H. Brown.

*No. XV.

Trinity Sunday.

"Holy, Holy, Holy."

OLY, blessed TRINITY,
Undivided UNITY,
Songs of praise we sing to Thee.

FATHER, our petitions hear,
Gentle JESU, be Thou near,
HOLY GHOST, our spirits cheer.

Meekly we Thy truth receive,
Help us ever to believe
And to Thee, our GOD, to cleave.

Three in One, and One in Three,
Glory, laud, and duty be
From Thy youthful family. Amen.

---

* Music by L. J. Turrell.

*No. XVI.

Children's Services.

"Out of the mouths of babes and sucklings Thou hast perfected praise."

O our Heavenly FATHER,
    We, His children, come;
    Seeking here His presence,
      In His Church, our home.
        Hear, accept, and bless us,
        Holy TRINITY.

Prayer and praise we offer,
    Psalms and hymns we sing,
Thanks for mercies giving,
    Heart and voice we bring.
      Hear, &c.

Here to serve and worship
    Thee, our GOD, we learn;
Here from earth to Heaven
    We are taught to turn.
      Hear, &c.

LORD, to serve Thee truly,
    Our young hearts prepare;
Make Thy children joyful
    In Thy House of prayer.
      Hear, &c.

---

* Music by Sir F. G. Ouseley, Bart.

*Hymns for Children's Festivals.

EDITED BY THE AUTHOR AND ARTHUR H. BROWN.

(The three first Hymns are printed in Canon Bouverie's "Children's Service of Prayer and Praise.")

† No. I.

On our Festal Day.

ON our festal day,
    In its bright array,
O gracious SAVIOUR to Thine House we come;
    Children's joy shall be
    Smiled upon by Thee,
Who, once a Child, didst share an earthly home.

    For all joys of earth,
    For our harmless mirth,
Our glad thanksgivings unto Thee we bring;
    Hear us while we raise
    Grateful songs of praise,
And children's lips proclaim the children's King.

    On all things we do
    Right and pure and true,
We know we may Thy heavenly blessing claim;
    As on sacred days,
    So in week-day ways,
O may we praise and glorify Thy Name.

---

* From a Children's Festival Service, copyright of Messrs. Curwen.
† Music by A. H. Brown.

Ever by our side,
Be our GOD and Guide,
Our hearts to cheer amid this world of woe;
Thus through life may we
Be upheld by Thee,
And onward on our way rejoicing go. Amen.

* No. II.

O Kind and Gentle Saviour.

O KIND and gentle SAVIOUR,
  Who art the children's Friend,
We pray Thee now receive us,
  Thy blessing on us send :
Our joys and all our sorrows
  Thou willest we should bring,
And lay them all before Thee,
  Our good and gracious King.

The weary and sin-laden
  In Thee do find their rest ;
And when in Thee rejoicing,
  Our joys are doubly blest.
Thou didst vouchsafe Thy presence
  On Cana's marriage day,
Now at our feast be present,
  Accept our festal lay.

To Thee, of old, their children
  The people came and brought :
From Thee Thy grace and favour
  For little ones they sought.

---

* Music by A. H. Brown.

And Thou didst not forbid them,
  For Thou art good and kind;
In Thee a loving SAVIOUR
  May we, Thy children, find.

Let not our ways and doings
  Dishonour Thy dear Name,
Nor words nor deeds of evil
  Our Christian calling shame.
Grant us Thy grace, that boldly
  We may our LORD confess:
While for all gifts Thou givest
  Thy holy Name we bless.

* **No. III.**

To Christ, our Heavenly King.

TO CHRIST, our Heavenly King,
  Our strains of joy we raise;
And glad hosannas sing
  On these our festive days.
Alleluia! Thy children here
To Thee draw near,
  Alleluia!

We joy with one accord
  To sing our festal songs;
Taught by Thy holy word
  That praise to Thee belongs.
Alleluia! We sing again
In sweet refrain,
  Alleluia!

---

* Music by A. H. Brown.

On all kind friends we pray
  Thy blessing Thou wilt send;
Spare them to us, that they
  Thy little flock may tend.
Alleluia! For all good gifts
Each voice uplifts
  Alleluia!

O LORD of life and love,
  When earthly joys are o'er,
With angel hosts above
  May we sing evermore
Alleluia! Be this our song
Through ages long.
  Alleluia! Amen.

Children's Hymns for Church Seasons.

Edited by the Author and Arthur H. Brown.

*No. I.
Christmas-tide.

Now once more we greet thee,
   Holy, happy morn;
With glad songs we meet thee,
   For to us is born
One so meek and lowly,
   One Who asks our love;
Yet so high and holy,
   From the realms above.

One Who came to save us
   From the guilt of sin,
One Whose dying gave us
   Strength the goal to win;
Once as babes they brought us
   To that Saviour dear,
Ever since they taught us
   To believe Him near.

Full of joy and gladness
   Is our Christmas-tide,
Comfort in our sadness,
   By its hopes supplied.
Of earth's many voices
   None such joy impart,
As when now rejoices
   Every Christian heart.

---

* Music by Sir J. Stainer.

Thou didst come to win us
From each sinful way,
And to dwell within us
Through life's little day.
JESU, go before us
As we journey on,
From that throne watch o'er us
Whither Thou art gone. Amen.

* No. II.

Christmas Carol.

GATHER, Christian children,
On this happy day,
Yours to greet the Infant LORD,
Yours to tune the lay.

For the sake of children
To this earth He came,
Theirs the tribute now to bring—
Praising His dear Name.

Children their Hosannas
To the lowly King
Sang to greet Him, as He rode,
Meekly triumphing.

In His arms He took them
With a fond caress:
Children ever dear to Him
JESUS still doth bless.

---

* Prize Carol. Music by A. H. Brown. Copyright of "Sunday School Union."

Come then, Christian children,
On His Natal Day,
At the Crib of Bethlehem
Your meet homage pay.

* No. III.

Holy Innocents' Day.

FIRSTLINGS of martyrs to whom it was given
In your sweet innocence glory to win;
What if for loss of you sad hearts were riven,
Blessings for ever were then to begin.

Ye in your babyhood near your dear SAVIOUR
When upon earth He once "came to His own";
Near to Him still ye are, near Him for ever,
Faultless He places you round His bright throne.

JESU, Who unto Thee tookest the children,
Lovingly, tenderly into Thine arms,
We will adore Thee, praise Thee, and pray to Thee,
Bless us and shield us from sin's dire alarms.

Lead us, Thy little flock, good and kind Shepherd,
For Thou art merciful, mighty to save;
Lead Thou us onward, beside the still waters,
With Thee we triumph o'er death and the grave.

---

* Music by A. H. Brown.

* No. IV.

Epiphany-tide.

ROM our childhood's early years
    We have heard of that bright star
Sent to be a guide to Thee,
    JESU, LORD, from lands afar.

By its rays the wise men led
    On their long and weary way,
Came their precious gifts to bring,
    Lowly worship came to pay.

Gold they gave to Thee as King,
    Token of Thy future throne;
Frankincense—as to their GOD,
    Myrrh—Thy precious death did own.

What we have Thou gavest us,
    May it ever be our joy—
Life and health and time, yea all
    In Thy service to employ. Amen.

† No. V.

Easter-tide.

LET hosannas ring while the children sing
    Of the LORD's Easter victory;
How from out the gloom of that garden tomb
    Life and Light He came forth to be.
        O bless us to-day, LORD JESU,
            As we come to rejoice in Thee.

---

* Music by T. Morley.   † Music by Rev. T. R. Matthews.

When the LORD arose from His brief repose,
    Then He set all His people free;
For the galling yoke of our foe He broke,
    And He gained us our liberty.
        O bless us to-day, &c.

LORD, to us give grace unto Thee to live,
    And to die unto sin in Thee;
If in Thee we die, then beyond the sky
    We shall live through eternity.
        O bless us to-day, &c.

* No. VI.

Ascension=tide.

JESUS from above
  Once came down in love
From His bright eternal dwelling,
By His advent gloom dispelling,
  Making glad this earth
  By His wondrous birth.

  To yon realms on high,
  Far above the sky,
Jesus Christ, our Lord, ascended,
All His human sorrows ended,
  There at GOD's right hand
  Faith can see Him stand.

---

* Set to music by Rev. Canon F. A. J. Hervey.

Thither He once more,
All His labours o'er,
Has gone up: now interceding,
For His children He is pleading,
Till He come again
Over all to reign.

Praises then we sing
To the ascended King,
As we tell the heavenly story,
As we sing the Victor's glory,
At His Name we bow,
Crowned in triumph now. Amen.

* No. VII.

Whitsun=tide.

DAY of wonders, day of gladness,
    When the SPIRIT came,
  On the saintly heads descended
    Tongues of flame.

And the heavenly wind came rushing
  With a mighty sound,
While the HOLY GHOST was filling
  All around.

They CHRIST'S promise were awaiting,
  That first Whitsun-day;
To His word we still are looking,
  E'en as they.

---

* Music by A. H. Brown.

Holy Comforter, we pray Thee
In our hearts abide,
As through life Thy children wander,
Be our Guide.

✠

* No. VIII.

Trinity=tide.

HOLY TRINITY, for ever blessèd,
UNITY of Love Divine,
With favour look on us Thy children,
Make us pure, and keep us Thine;
In that most sacred Name adopted,
Once made members of the SON,
By grace still may we be defended,
While on earth our race we run.
Holy TRINITY, for ever blessèd
UNITY of Love Divine,
With favour look on us Thy children,
Make us pure, and keep us Thine.

Holy FATHER, merciful CREATOR,
Thou to us our life dost give;
In Thee alone we have our being,
For by Thee all creatures live;
O JESU, Thou Who dost redeem us,
We would love Thee and adore,
O HOLY GHOST, our Sanctifier,
Lead and guide us evermore.
Holy TRINITY, for ever blessèd,
UNITY of Love Divine,
With favour look on us Thy children,
Heal our souls, for we are Thine.

---

* Music by A. H. Brown.

Holy TRIUNE GOD, for our salvation,
　In Thy love for each one's soul,
Three Holy Persons were united,
　May that love still make us whole;
O keep Thy children, prone to wander
　And forsake the narrow way;
We need Thee ever to restore us
　To the fold from whence we stray.
　　Holy TRINITY, for ever blessèd,
　　　UNITY of Love Divine,
　　With favour look on us Thy children,
　　　Guard Thou us, and keep us Thine.

* No. IX.

Harvest=tide.

JOYFUL is the Harvest-tide,
　　To men GOD's good gifts bringing,
　Old and young their songs unite,
　　Their FATHER'S praises singing;
O'er the world He scatters gifts
　In rich abundant measure,
Never does His promise fail,
　Earth yields its golden treasure.
　　Praise we GOD with grateful hearts
　　　For gifts men have been storing,
　　Yearly to His House we come,
　　　The Harvest's LORD adoring.

---

* Music by A. H. Brown.

For our life and breath and health
  And food on Him depending,
Who the sunshine and the rain
  To earth is ever sending;
Blade and ear shoot forth and spring,
  But how—no mortal knoweth,
Day by day, and night by night,
  The tender corn-stalk groweth.
    Praise we GOD with grateful hearts
      For gifts men have been storing,
    Yearly to His House we come,
      The Harvest's LORD adoring.

Yet far richer food than this
  Our GOD and FATHER giveth,
Bread of Heaven, our staff and stay,
  On this the spirit liveth.
Ever, LORD, give us this bread,
  As through the desert dreary
Thy pilgrim children onward press,
  All faint and weak and weary.
    Praise we GOD with grateful hearts
      For all good gifts He sendeth,
    Food for body, food for soul,
      For life that never endeth.

Carols.

*Christmas Carols.

† No. I.
The Angelic Salutation.

A PARAPHRASE FROM THE HOLY GOSPELS.

"Nowel-el el el,
Now is wel that evere was voo."—C. A.D. 1460.

HAIL! thou that art so highly graced, ‡
  To thee I bring this word,
Among all women blest art thou,
  For with Thee is the LORD:
Let not Thy spirit troubled be,
  And be not thou afraid,
For thou with GOD dost favour find,
  Then be not thou dismay'd.

Hail thou! for by the HOLY GHOST
  Thou shalt a Son conceive:
Then, prithee, Mary, calm thy fears,
  Only this word believe:—
"Then shall a Virgin be with Child,"
  So did GOD's seer tell,
And men confessing Him shall find
  Their true EMMANUEL.

---

* The music to all Carols was either composed or arranged by Mr. A. H. Brown.

† Published in "Newbery House Magazine," A.D. 1891.

‡ "κεχαριτωμένη." "Salve, Deo grata ac dilecta, a Deo summis beneficiis afficienda."—*Schleusner.*

And JESUS be His Holy Name,
    All other names above,
Adored in Heaven and in earth
    The SAVIOUR, LORD of love:
SON of the Highest shall He be,
    In Him mankind shall own
A Prince, henceforth to occupy
    His father David's throne.

And o'er the house of Jacob, He
    Dominion shall extend,
And of His Kingdom there shall be
    From this time forth no end:
The SPIRIT of the LORD Supreme
    His handmaid shall come nigh,
Thine Holy Offspring shall be styled
    The SON OF GOD Most High.

* No. II.

Brothers, ye must Merry be.

BROTHERS, ye must merry be
    At this joyous season,
In this our society
Now all contrariety
    We account as treason.

---

* Written to an old German Melody (beginning of sixteenth century). Published in " Penny Post," A.D. 1887.

For a Master we do own
  High in Heaven above us,
Who on earth a little Child
Was so lowly, meek, and mild,
  Who did greatly love us.

With the love He bore to us
  We must love each other.
In our Confraternity
There must peace and concord be,
  While dislikes we smother.

'Tis the season to forgive,
  'Tis the time of gladness.
Grudges—let them perish now,
Right goodwill we cherish now,
  Banish'd be all sadness.

Hail the happy Christmas-tide,
  Welcome be it ever!
Each his place must now be taking,
To enhance our merry-making,
  Doing his endeavour.

*No. III.

Come, meek Souls, whose lot is lowly.

COME, meek souls, whose lot is lowly,
    Ye must tune the lay,
Hymning now the gladsome tidings
    Of this Festal Day.
Come, for unto humble shepherds,
    Watching o'er their fold,
Was vouchsafed the heav'nly vision
    In those days of old.

Meet it was to these the Angel
    Should proclaim His birth,
Who in heart was meek and lowly
    All His days on earth;
Yet to Him, throned in high Heaven,
    They are bidden come,
Who, content His steps to follow,
    Make not earth their home.

Sing ye, "Glory in the Highest,"
    Sing the Prince of Peace,
Come, proclaim "Good-will to all men,"
    In the world's release.
Come and laud ye GOD the FATHER,
    Who did send His SON,
Come, adore the Infant JESUS,
    With the FATHER One.

---

* Words adapted to a German melody. Published in "Church Bells," A.D. 1887.

*No. IV.

Come One and All.

"Thy welcome Eve, loved Christmas now arrived,
The parish bells their tuneful peal resound,
And mirth and gladness every breast pervade."
—ROMAINE JOSEPH THORNE, A.D. 1780.

COME one and all, come great and small,
    Come lad and lass, come sire and son,
It is our Christmas Festival,
    And absent there must be not one!
Now right good cheer shall crown the year,
    Whilst kith and kin do gather round:
From all the steeples far and near
    A peal of welcome shall resound.

And now once more to rich and poor
    "Glad tidings of great joy" are come,
While all within the old Church door
    Can seek and find one common home.
There each can raise his strain of praise
    To hail the LORD'S Nativity:
Like Angel-hosts in olden days
    Poured forth harmonious minstrelsy.

These anthems o'er, oft sung of yore,
    That waken joy at Noel-tide,
The feast is spread in bounteous store,
    The rich man's gates are open wide:
And hearty wishes now go round
    That happiness may crown the day,
And still in coming years abound,
    When Father Christmas holds his sway.

---

* Published in "In Excelsis Gloria." "Carols for Christmas-tide," A.D. 1885.

*No. V.
Let Christians all Rejoice and Sing.

LET Christians all rejoice and sing,
Their strains of hearty welcome bring,
Now we hail CHRIST's Natal Day;
Praise! Praise!
Joy of joys to men alway,
CHRIST the joy of souls forlorn,
CHRIST the LORD of all is born.
Hail this happy day!

Let Christians all rejoice and sing,
Their strains of hearty welcome bring,
Tidings glad for all mankind;
All, all,
In that manger solace find,
Doubts and fears are laid to rest,
Hope springs up in each one's breast,
Hope for all mankind.

Let Christians all rejoice and sing,
Their strains of hearty welcome bring,
To greet the Babe of Bethlehem;
Aye, aye,
Fairest shoot of Jesse's stem,
This for aye our song shall be,
CHRIST and His Nativity,
Babe of Bethlehem.

---

* Published in "The Church Musician," A.D. 1871.

*No. VI.
Long look'd for Morn.

LONG look'd for Morn! what dawn so bright
  E'er broke from Eastern portals?
All hail the day! Henceforth alway
  So dear to grateful mortals.
    Joy, joy, this Christmas Morn!
    The SAVIOUR of the world is born:
    Wake, wake once more to laud
    The Virgin-born REDEEMER!

Come, gather, Christian people, all,
  This is a day of gladness;
With anthems meet, the LORD we greet,
  There is no room for sadness.
    Joy, joy, &c.

No natal day e'er dawn'd like this,
  When, cradled in a manger,
He slept in peace. No age shall cease
  To glorify the Stranger.
    Joy, joy, &c.

No morn on earth shall ever break
  So fraught with consolation,
Until, once more, when time is o'er,
  Shall come man's full salvation.
    Now, now, this Christmas Morn,
    In low estate is JESUS born;
    Then, then, all eyes shall see
    The LORD in all His glory.

---

* Published in "Joy and Gladness" Christmas Carols, with music of the olden time by A. H. Brown and S. Childs Clarke.

*No. VII.

Once Again the Holy Season.

ONCE again the Holy Season
    Comes with gladness in its train;
Once again with hearts and voices
    Join we in the sweet refrain
Erstwhile by angelic minstrels
    Chanted—ever welcome still:
"Unto GOD on high be glory;
    Peace on earth, to men goodwill!"

What though dull and dreary winter
    Bind the earth with icy chain,
And each brightly-flowing streamlet
    Cease to course along the plain,
All is warm within the homestead;
    Hearts with joy this strain must fill:
"Unto GOD on high be glory;
    Peace on earth, to men goodwill!"

† "From above, drop down, ye Heavens,
    Righteousness from out the skies;
For, from earth springs up Salvation"—
    GOD's dear SON in human guise.
Wondrous love to stoop so humbly
    His great mission to fulfil:
"Unto GOD on high be glory;
    Peace on earth, to men goodwill!"

---

* Published in "New and Old," A.D. 1890.
† Isaiah xlv. 8.

'Twas for us, His wayward children,
    CHRIST His glory laid aside;
'Twas for us Himself He humbled,
    When on earth He lived and died.
Heaven's anthems—songs of Angels—
    Childlike hearts shall ever thrill:
"Unto GOD on high be glory;
    Peace on earth, to men goodwill!"

* No. VIII.

O Deep was the Gloom.

DEEP was the gloom hanging over the earth,
    Gross darkness had shrouded the land,
When Angels did herald the LORD's lowly birth
    In strains of their Heaven-taught band.
        To mortals forlorn now was open'd a door,
            For lowly and meek there were blessings
                in store,
        To every nation came news of salvation,
        Glad tidings for rich and for poor.

O strange was the token and bright was the gleam
    That beckon'd the Magi from far;
A light to the Gentiles Thy shining did seem,
    Thou beauteous and wonderful Star!
        To mortals forlorn, &c.

---

* Published in "Newbery House Magazine," A.D. 1889.

O Day-Star illumine each sin-stricken heart,
O Thou, Sun of Righteousness, rise,
Bid all the dread shadows of darkness depart—
The clouds hiding Thee from our eyes.
To mortals forlorn Thou dost open a door,
For lowly and meek Thou hast blessings in store,
To every nation Thou broughtest salvation,
Glad tidings to rich and to poor.

* No. IX.

The Quaternion of Seraphs. †

"*Drop down, ye heavens, from above, and let the skies pour down Righteousness: let the earth open, and let them bring forth Salvation, and let Righteousness spring up together.*"
—ISAIAH XLV. 8.

WELCOME morn of joy and gladness,
O'er a lost world dawning bright;
Angel hosts once kept its vigil
Carolling 'mid gloom of night.
Now is come the Great Salvation,
§ Now sin's captives find release,
Truth and mercy meet together,
Righteousness embraces Peace.

---

* Published in "Banner of Faith."

† See Dr. Hook's "Devout Musings on the Psalms."

§ "Solutâ captivitate, felicem populi statum designat, omni bonorum copiâ et virtutibus florentis: quæ maximè impleta sunt, postquam CHRISTUS — Ipsa Veritas — Idemque Pax nostra, e terrâ ortus est."—*Bossuet.*

Parted at the fall of Adam,
   Angel virtues long estranged,
Bethlehem beholds their meeting
   In sweet concord newly ranged.
"Bright quaternion of seraphs," †
   Never shall their union cease,
      Truth and Mercy met together,
      Righteousness embracing Peace.

CHRIST, in human form Incarnate,
   Springs as "Truth" from out the earth,
Righteousness looks down from Heaven
   Smiling on that wondrous Birth.
¶ Yea, the LORD shall rain down goodness,
   Blessings shall to earth increase,
      Truth with Mercy now united,
      Righteousness for aye with Peace.

*No. X.

The Brightest Day of all the Year.

FROM out the dim and distant past,
   Still handed on from sire to son,
Thy charm is destin'd still to last
   As potent as when first begun;
Once more we greet Thine advent here,
Thou brightest day of all the year.

¶ Psalm lxxxv. 1, 10, 11, 12. Proper Psalm for Christmas Day.

* Published, with music by A. H. Brown, in the "Musical Times," A.D. 1889.

Unfailing theme of minstrel's song,
  And ever 'mid earth's gloom so bright!
Adown the ages all along
  Encircl'd thou with halo light!
Men greet thee when thou dost appear
As brightest day of all the year.

Now fondest mem'ries cluster round
  Our hearths and homes, for there are met,
As tho' it were on hallow'd ground,
  The dreams of childhood ling'ring yet;
To young and old is ever dear
The brightest day of all the year.

O day of peace and right goodwill,
  O day of joy and guileless mirth,
Whose mandate myriad hearts obey
  Since thy "glad tidings" reach'd this earth;
Long may Posterity revere
Thee,—brightest day of all the year.

* No. XI.

There's a Day that Hearts of Children.

THERE'S a day that hearts of children
  Needs must cheer,
A day in happiest childhood
  Held most dear.
'Tis a day when Heav'n seems nearer,
  Earth more glad,
When sorrowing hearts no longer
  Can be sad.

---

* Published in "Church Bells," of December 4th, 1891.

For **Christ Jesus**, **Lord** of children,
    On that morn
Was in Bethlehem's poor manger
    For them born.
He, the mighty King of Angels,
    Then came down
To procure for them hereafter
    Each a crown.

To lead them on to the mansions
    In the sky,
To point them to priceless treasures
    Stor'd on high.
To bid them all be seeking
    Things above,
Where reigns their merciful **Father**—
    God of love.

Then hail we with glad thanksgiving
    Christmas Day,
And tune for the Infant **Saviour**
    Sweetest lay:
Our hearts, fill'd with adoration,
    We will raise,
Our lips shall the gentle **Jesus**
    Bless and praise.

*No. XII.

The Good Shepherd and the Wolf.

HUSH! for around the fold doth prowl
The ravening wolf with dismal howl!
From him the hireling oft doth flee,
Whose own the sheep are not, and he
No care for them doth entertain—
The hireling serveth but for gain.
Alas! alas! defenceless sheep,
When none around them watch do keep.
 Hark! how to all on earth who dwell,
 Angelic hosts with joy foretell
 The Shepherd Chief of Israel!

Long were the sheep to wolves a prey,
Long was the "dark and cloudy day"; †
None did the cruel spoilers brave,
Nor pastors sought the flocks to save.
On mountains bleak they wandered far,
To search and find them none there are:
Is there no shepherd who will come
To fetch again the wanderers home?
 Hark! how, &c.

Lo, shepherds watching in the plain!
They hear a sweet entrancing strain,
Proclaiming One Who now is born,
Chief Shepherd of the sheep forlorn:
He shall be Victor in the strife,
But for His sheep lay down His life;
When He the ravening wolf shall see,
He will not, like the hireling, flee.
 Hark! how, &c.

---

* Published in "The Gospeller."   † Ezekiel xxxiv. 12.

Beside still waters He shall lead
His sheep that in green pastures feed;
No evil longer need they fear,
In utmost danger He is near.
His rod and staff shall comfort prove,
Guided and guarded by His love;
All perils of their wanderings o'er,
They shall be safe for evermore.
    Hark! how, &c.

* No. XIII.

The Weary World was Hush'd in Sleep.

THE weary world was hush'd in sleep,
But faithful swains their vigils keep,
When in the sky a vision bright
Broke in upon the gloom of night.
    Sing praise to GOD—to men be peace,
    From sin's dire thrall is found release;
    Once more shall Righteousness have birth,
    For Truth shall spring from out the earth.

Lo! minstrelsy of sweetest strain
Entranced their ears and filled the plain,
An angel choir their voices raise
To swell the dulcet song of praise.
    Sing praise to GOD, &c.

---

* Published in "The Gospeller," 1889.

Eye ne'er had seen a sight so fair,
Ear ne'er had heard so sweet an air:
Those welcome tidings chanted then
Shall cheer for aye the sons of men.
    Sing praise to GOD, &c.

From age to age, at Noel-tide,
Shall peace in grateful hearts abide;
And men shall echo o'er and o'er
The song that angels sang of yore.
    Sing praise to GOD, &c.

* No. XIV.

This World of ours was Beautiful.

"Welcome all wonders in one sight,
Eternity shut in a span:
Summer in winter, day in night,
Heaven in earth, and God in man!
Great Little One, Whose all-embracing birth,
Lifts earth to Heaven, stoops Heaven to earth."
    —RICHARD CRASHAW, A.D. 1615.

THIS world of ours was beautiful
    Despite the reign of sin,
    But lovelier far it all became
    When Christmas did begin;
When Heaven's bright angelic host
    Pour'd forth sweet minstrelsy,
Of peace on earth and right goodwill
    The harbinger to be.

---

* To music known as " S. Stephen's Carol."

When shepherds, by an angel taught,
    To Bethlehem did wend
Their way, and humbly there before
    The new-born babe did bend,
And then the Eastern Magi came
    From Araby afar,
To pay their lowly homage there
    Led by that guiding star.

A new creation took its date
    From that auspicious day!
The Second Adam then was born
    Who did new life convey;
Then earth and sea, and sky and air
    More beautiful became,
When fallen mortals learned to laud
    And bless CHRIST JESU'S Name.

Thee, Prince of Peace, they then did hail,
    Whose Birth-day ever brings
Remembrance of the "Sun that rose
    With healing on His wings,"
And light and warmth and "fire of love"
    His genial rays impart :—
O, gentle JESU, be Thou born
    To-day within each heart.

* No. XV.
We Sing a Mighty Wonder.

WE sing a mighty wonder,
 A tale of joy we tell;
A tale, though told so often,
 Good Christians love so well.
A tale once heard from Heaven
 In ages long ago,
Heard by the lowly shepherds
 Who watch'd their flocks below.
  O happy, happy tidings,
   Brought to a world forlorn;
  That on this blessed morning
   JESUS our LORD was born.

A tale the Angel told them
 To hand from age to age,
A tale they heard rejoicing,
 That must all hearts engage.
For them the herald Angel
 Such marvels did unfold,
Such tidings of great gladness
 Ne'er yet to mortals told.
  O happy, happy tidings, &c.

At last the promis'd SAVIOUR
 To this lone world was come,
Who left the joys of Heaven
 To make this earth His home.
Now Truth and Mercy meeting,
 Man's true joy shall increase,
And now the blissful greeting
 'Twixt Righteousness and Peace.
  O happy, happy tidings, &c.

---

* Published in "New and Old," and in "Our Waifs and Strays."

No. XVI.

With Wary Steps Approach We.

WITH wary steps approach we
    Once more the manger throne—
For there the Infant JESUS
    Our GOD and King we own,
The Covenant of Mercy
    Is ratified to-day;
Its sweet and wondrous lessons
    Lo! there He doth display.*
    O dawn of changeless glory!
        From Eastern skies it springs;
    Earth's Christmas SUN is rising
        With healing in His wings.

Adore we, with the angels,
    The LORD of life and love,
In lowly guise appearing
    On earth, from realms above.
He comes, from sin's dire thraldom
    Its captives to release;
He comes, rich gifts to offer—
    His pardon, grace, and peace.
    O dawn, &c.

---

* " Entrons tous dans l'étable,
    Là, nous instruira l'enfant JESUS:
    Là, on lit pêle-mêle
    Le Nouveau Testament vraiment,
    C'en est l'enseignement."
        —*Ancient French Carol.*

And shall we not prepare Him
  Within our hearts a place,
When each is sorely needing
  The comforts of His grace,
Who once, for our salvation,
  In Bethlehem was born,
When Heaven's angelic minstrels
  Did usher in the morn!
    O dawn, &c.

* No. XVII.

When Father Christmas Comes.

ALL hail the time of gladness,
  The gladdest of the year!
Should there be aught of sadness
  When Noel-tide is here?
Goodwill must fill all hearts and merriment our homes,
  When with his jocund train
  Old Father Christmas comes.

Now is the time of singing
  The winsome strains of yore,
Now is the time of bringing
  Good cheer among the poor.
Goodwill must fill all hearts and merriment our homes,
  When with his jocund train
  Old Father Christmas comes.

---

* Published in "Newbery House Magazine," A.D. 1891.

Now is the time of meeting
　Of friends from far and near,
Now is the time of greeting
　The absent ones so dear.
Hence all estrangement now from English hearts and homes,
　When with his jocund train
　Old Father Christmas comes.

* No. XVIII.

Noël.

WAKE once more a joyous strain,
　Sing we Noël once again,
　　While our EMMANUEL we bless!
All grateful homage bringing,
　　Loud Hosannas singing—
Praise we now the Infant King,
Let our acclamations ring,
Laud we now in exultation
Him Who comes to bring salvation—
　JESUS CHRIST our Righteousness.
　　Angels greet Him in the sky,
　　Let us to their songs reply;
　　O Love all love excelling,
　　GOD makes with man His dwelling.

Well a guilty world might fear
Tidings from on high to hear;
　Yet Heaven's windows do not ope
With floods of vengeance sweeping
　　Over mortals weeping:

---

* From a Service of Song, "Christmas-tide," placed on the S.P.C.K. Supplemental Catalogue.

P

Nor with Sodom's showers of fire,
Nor in Sinai's accents dire,
But with utmost sweetness sounding,
With celestial peace abounding,
  Wakening love and faith and hope.
      Angels greet, &c.

Now has dawned earth's brightest morn,
For the SAVIOUR CHRIST is born;
  He is the Bright and Morning Star,
The whole wide world rejoices!
  Lift your hearts and voices.
Praise ye now th' Incarnate Word,
Praise your everlasting LORD;
Mortals, sing in exultation!
Raised from deepest degradation
  All His ransomed people are.
      Angels greet, &c.

✠

No. XIX.

𝔜ᵉ Shepherd of 𝔜ᵉ Shepherds.

FROM out the spacious firmament,
  Amid the gloom of night,
  With many a glitt'ring gem besprent,
  Appears a wondrous sight:
'Twas where of old good Jesse's son
  His flocks did tend and keep,

---

* "David was once a shepherd at Bethlehem, and doubtless often watched his father Jesse's sheep on these same pastures."— *The Bishop of Bedford's Commentary (S.P.C.K.) on S. Luke ii.* 8.

The Angel told of joy begun,
　To those who watch'd their sheep.
　　Hail, thou the heav'n-sent harbinger!
　　　Good tidings thou dost bring;
　　　And year by year in carol clear
　　　That gladsome news we sing.

And David's Son in Bethlehem
　The shepherds now might see;
Henceforth true Pastor He to them
　And all the world would be:
King David was a watchful swain
　Ere raised to fill a throne,
Now David's Royal Son must reign,
　Yet watches o'er His own.
　　And so we hail the harbinger
　　　Who did those tidings bring;
　　　And year by year with carol clear
　　　That gladsome news we sing.

No shepherd e'er such tender care
　Of wand'ring sheep could take
As He, Who, loving, did not spare
　His life-blood for their sake;
O Shepherd of Thine Israël,
　Of Whom the Angel told,
In pastures safe lead us to dwell
　For ever in Thy fold.
　　We hail to-day that harbinger
　　　Who did these tidings bring;
　　　And year by year with carol clear
　　　That gladsome news we sing.

✠

*No. XX.

A Virgin did Come.

A VIRGIN did come from lowliest home,
    And shelter she fain in a manger would find ;
For full was the inn, and no room was within,
Save where to the stalls the mute oxen they bind.
    O how wondrous the love and the deep humility
    Of Him Who was laid in that manger for me.

That Babe was a King, mystic gifts, lo, they bring!
    Sure tokens they were of some great One to be;
To Bethlehem led, Eastern princes had sped
    From afar "The Desire of all Nations" to see.
        O how wondrous, &c.

Accomplished their hope, their treasures they ope—
    Gold, frankincense, myrrh, to that Infant they brought,
Gifts costly and rare, full of meaning they were
    Tho' not yet unveil'd were the great truths they taught.
        O how wondrous, &c.

No tokens of state round that Royal Babe wait,
    Seeming least, and yet greatest of monarchs was He ;
But in reverence low princely Magi did bow,
    As tho' they divin'd all His true dignity.
        O how wondrous, &c.

---

* Written to a melody of the Seventeenth Century.

*A New Year's Carol.

"What think ye? A certain man had two sons; and he came to the first and said, Son, go work to-day in my vineyard. He answered and said, I will not; but afterwards he repented, and went. And he came to the second, and said likewise. And he, answering, said, I go, Sir, and went not. Whether of these twain did the will of his father?"—S. MATT. XXI. 28-31.

WAKE and sing the New Year's Advent,
   O ye children of the day,
Looking back and looking forward
   As the fleet years pass away:
Gird your loins for fresh endeavour,
   While endeavour yet ye may.

For the days are flitting past you
   As they vanish one by one;
And life's battle is not ended,
   And life's goal is not yet won:
"Son, go work thou in My vineyard,"
   Ere the working hours be done.

What if, hitherto, the answer
   "I will not" has long been thine:
In the parable thou readest
   How of this—his mood supine—
That "first" son, in time repenting,
   Did to honest toil incline.

Shun we, then, all false profession:
   Of our work the world hath need:—
Not alone to cry, "I go, Sir!"
   While of toil I take no heed:
Let this be our New Year's motto—
   "ALL TRUE WORKERS GOD WILL SPEED."

---

* Published in "The Church Monthly," A.D. 1889.

Easter Carols.

*No. I.

Awake, Awake, with Holy Rapture Sing

"Out of the strong came forth sweetness."—JUDGES XIV. 14.

    AWAKE, awake, with holy rapture sing
        The Risen LORD.
    Earth knows of no such joy
    So free from base alloy:
    And Heaven's hosts unite
    To greet a morn so bright.
        Awake, awake, &c.

Proclaim, proclaim the ever-welcome morn,
    The Paschal Feast—
The LAMB OF GOD once slain
This day we hail again:
The Passover we keep,
No longer mourn nor weep.
    Proclaim, &c.

Rejoice, rejoice the Conqueror to greet,
    His conquest won!
From Judah's Lion torn
Is source of sweetness born:
The sweet springs from the strong,
Be this our Paschal Song.
    Rejoice, rejoice the Conqueror to greet,
        His conquest won! Alleluia!

---

* Published in "Church Bells."

* No. II.

Awake, My Glory.

"To the end that my glory may sing praise unto Thee, and not be silent; O Lord, my God, I will give thanks unto Thee for ever."—PSALM XXX. 12. †

AWAKE, ‡ my glory, harp, and lute,
    I will awake
  Right early,—let no tongue be mute,
    Each now his part must take.
Sound forth once more the Victor's song,
    Yea, let there be
Thanksgiving heard His Courts among,
    And voice of melody.
              Alleluia!

Bring forth the flowers of genial Spring
    Blooming anew;
Raise your triumphal strains and sing
    That JESUS rose for you.
For you He agonised and died,
    For you He lives,
For you life from His piercèd side
    The cleansing Fountain gives.
              Alleluia!

---

* Published in "Penny Post." Music by A. H. Brown.

† The end of CHRIST's Resurrection, of the salvation of the souls of the faithful, and the resurrection of their bodies, is one and the same, namely, the glory of GOD, Who is the Author of every kind of deliverance, Whose praise should therefore be resounded by the grateful tongues of the redeemed from generation to generation; as the tongue then becometh the "glory" of man when it is employed in setting forth the glory of GOD.—*Bishop Horne, on Psalm xxx.*

‡ *Idem* on Psalm lvii. 8, 9, 10, 11—the Second Psalm for Easter Day.

* Among the people evermore
Shall echo praise,
As in the distant days of yore,
On this bright Day of days:
* For unto Heaven above doth rise
His mercy great,
Eternal truth beyond the skies
Our souls shall celebrate.
Alleluia !

✠

† No. III.

Awhile the Victor Vanquish'd Lay.

AWHILE the Victor vanquish'd lay—
From weakness e'en the stronger;
His heel though bruisèd in the fray,
His foe prevails no longer.
Let each one now his carol bring,
For each may now in triumph sing,
He hath for us the conquest won,
Who is "The Resurrection."

Hark! hear the Vanquisher proclaim,
"Lo, I am He Who liveth;"
Once numbered with the dead—the Same
Who life to mortals giveth.
Let each one now, &c.

* *Idem* on Psalm lvii. 8, 9, 10, 11—the Second Psalm for Easter Day.

† From "Easter-tide," a Service of Sacred Song, and "The Gospeller," A.D. 1884.

    His struggle past, his conflict o'er,
      Death's prison-keys he holdeth ;
    "Henceforth alive for evermore,"
      Life's pathway He unfoldeth.
        Let each one now, &c.

*No. IV.

Come, for the Night of Gloom is o'er.

COME, for the night of gloom is o'er
    And ended Lenten sadness:
Come, for the Easter sun once more
    Doth waken earth to gladness.
      Bright the Day-spring in the East,
      Therefore let us keep the feast.

Come in the early morning hour—
    Uplift your hearts and voices ;
Come, for the storm-clouds cease to lower ;
    Earth now in spring rejoices.
      Bright the Day-spring, &c.

Come, on this Resurrection morn,
    With JESU'S presence o'er us ;
He breathes again our breath, new-born
    He goeth on before us.
      Bright the Day-spring, &c.

Come, for the Paschal LAMB is slain,
    The types and shadows ended :
When CHRIST our LORD did rise again,
    Then earth with Heaven was blended.
      Bright the Day-spring, &c.

---

* Published in "The Gospeller," A.D. 1889.

*No. V.

Hail! All Hail this Brightest Morning.

"I went with them to the House of God, with the voice of joy and praise, with a multitude that kept holyday."—PSALM XLII. 4.

HAIL! all hail this brightest morning!
Lo, the glorious Easter sun
Earth with golden light adorning,
As "his course he joys to run." †
Nature, winter gloom forsaking,
Spring, anew dominion taking,
Is begun.

Ended now the night of weeping:
Joyous in her bright array
Holy-day the Church is keeping,
Dear to Christian hearts alway.
Yester eve had Jesus rested
Ere with glory He invested
Each Lord's Day.

Triumph of the Victor singing
On this "Queen of festal days,"
To His Courts our tribute bringing,
Carol we His worthy praise.
Christ is risen! Christ is risen!
He hath burst His rock-bound prison!
Hearts upraise.
Alleluia! Alleluia! Alleluia!

---

* Published in "Penny Post," A.D. 1888, and in "New and Old," A.D. 1896.

† Psalm xix. 4, 5, 6.

No. VI.

Hence all Sorrow, Hence your Fear.

"*Go tell My brethren that I go before them.*"

* "*Both He that sanctifieth, and they who are sanctified, are all of One: for which cause He is not ashamed to call them Brethren.*"—HEBREWS ii. 11.

HENCE all sorrow! Hence your fear!
    Angel voices say,
  This glad morn, to Christians dear,
    Ushers in the day—
When the LORD in mercy meets them,
With His sweet compassion greets them,
He, henceforth, as brethren treats them—
    Hear Him, brothers, say—
"Be not afraid: Go tell My brethren that
    I go before them."

Wondrous love, to stoop so low,
    Like to men to be!
Teach, O LORD, our hearts to glow,
    As we hear from Thee,
After death and bitter passion,
Found once more in human fashion,
In Thine infinite compassion,
    Message full and free—
    "Be not afraid," &c.

---

* "He, their risen LORD, would take away all the 'fear,' and leave only 'the great joy.' . . . What love was in the word 'brethren'!"—*Bishop Walsham How's Commentary, S.P.C.K.*

For not only didst Thou go
    Into Galilee,
That Thy "little flock" might know
    Thy fond charity,
But Thou goest on before us,
Still Thy rod and staff are o'er us,
Till in Paradise Thou store us:
    Yes, we hear from Thee—
        "Be not afraid," &c.

* No. VII.

𝔐𝔞𝔫 𝔒𝔢 𝔯𝔬𝔰𝔢, 𝔰𝔦𝔫𝔠𝔢 𝔐𝔞𝔫 𝔒𝔢 𝔡𝔦𝔢𝔡.
(After S. Ambrose.)

"*Behold My hands and My feet, that it is I myself: handle Me, and see; for a spirit hath not flesh and bones, as ye see Me have.*"—S. Luke xxiv. 39.

MAN He rose, since Man He died. †
Man for men—the Crucified!
Known as Man to men before,
Known as mortal Man no more.
His Manhood quickenèd for us must be,
Henceforth the Quickener Himself is He.

    To His flesh all creatures owe
    Priceless gifts He doth bestow:
    Christ the First-fruits—Christ their Head,
    First begotten from the dead.
        His Manhood quickenèd, &c.

---

* Published in "The Gospeller."

† "One shall say unto Him, What are these wounds in Thine hands? Then He shall answer, Those with which I was wounded in the House of My friends."—*Zech. xiii.* 6.

All things rose in Him again,
All things 'neath His sway remain:
Earth and Heaven shall be new,
He Creation doth renew.
    His Manhood quickenèd, &c.

Lo! He takes again His life—
Victor in the deadly strife;
Life He yielded for us all,
Death no more can men enthral.
His Manhood quickenèd for us must be,
Henceforth the Quickener Divine is He.

* No. VIII.

'Mid the Loveliness of Spring-tide.

"Then were the disciples glad when they saw the Lord."

'MID the loveliness of Spring-tide,
    'Mid the incense of the flow'rs,
    'Mid new strains of feather'd songsters,
    O'er this nether world of ours,
'Mid the sights and sounds of beauty,
    From earth's gloom all newly born,
With its tale of joy and gladness
    Breaks the glorious Easter Morn!

O that morn of fadeless splendour!
    O that dawn of endless day!
Sun of Righteousness, then rising,
    Thou didst chase death's shades away.

---

* Published in "New and Old," A.D. 1888.

Ever with unearthly brightness
　Thou dost shed Thy dazzling rays,
Still to gild anew the dawning
　Of this day—the Day of days.

With a glad and holy rapture,
　In those distant days of old,
Did Thy faithful ones, adoring,
　Their dear LORD once more behold :
So we, too, with hearts elated,
　Can be now nor sad nor lorn,
As we sing of JESUS risen
　On this glorious Easter Morn !

* No. IX.

Morning Joy.

"And He shall be as the Light of the morning, when the sun riseth, even a morning without clouds : as the tender grass springing out of the earth by clear shining after rain." "These be the last words of David."—2 SAMUEL XXIII. 4.

"At even-tide weeping comes to lodge, but at morn is joy." †
　　　　　　　　—DR. KAY, ON PSALM XXX. 5.

THE "Daughters of Jerusalem"
　　Their ‡ mournful vigil kept,
And in lone sadness sorrowing,
　　The LORD's disciples wept.
　　§ Tho' heaviness, unwelcome guest,
　　　　May tarry for the night,
　　　Yet leaving, must give place to joy
　　　　That comes with morning light.

---

* Published in "The Gospeller," A.D. 1891.

† "The sorrow is but a wanderer, who has a lodging given him for the night, and must leave next morning."—*Note from Bourdillon's " Cloudy Days." S.P.C.K.*

‡ Matt. xxvii. 61.　　　§ Psalm xxx. 5.

Hence, all sad memories, for now
  Amid the vernal skies,
With healing on His golden wings *
  Yon Easter Sun doth rise.
    Tho' heaviness, &c.

"As Light of morning shall He be, †
  As cloudless dawn again
Breaks forth upon the dripping bowers
  Clear shining after rain."
    Tho' heaviness, &c.

What tho' in tears He sowed His seed, ‡
  Full sheaves shall bring Him joy;
The travail of His suffering soul
  Wrought bliss without alloy.
    Tho' heaviness, &c.

The "First-fruits" He of them that sleep §
  Amid Time's furrowed fields:
The "Wave-sheaf"—token of the store ∥
  Earth's last great Harvest yields.
    Tho' heaviness, &c.

---

* Mal. iv. 2.   † 2 Sam. xxiii. 4.   ‡ Psalm cxxvi. 5, 6.
  § 1 Cor. xv. 23.   ∥ Lev. xxiii. 10, 11.

* No. X.

O Day of all Days.

"They that dwell under His Shadow shall return; they shall revive as the corn, and grow as the vine."

 DAY of all days—far the sweetest and brightest
    That ever yet dawn'd on this woe-stricken earth;
O Morn of all morns, all the world thou delightest,
    Proclaiming to mortals thine angel-taught mirth.
      We greet thee, happy, Heavenly Festival!
        Nor death nor grave can now our souls enthral.

O long was the night in deep heaviness shrouded
    Ere JESUS had risen to scatter the gloom,
And gross was the darkness this earth had o'erclouded
    Ere Life, Light, and Glory burst forth from the tomb.
      We greet Thee, &c.

He cometh again Who in sad tears was sowing,
    His harvest to gather in fulness of joy;
His sheaves ever bringing and safely bestowing,
    Where blight and corruption no more can destroy.
      We greet Thee, &c.

LORD JESU, First-fruits of the faithful departed,
    The Wave-sheaf denoting the Harvest to come;
Consoler Supreme of the sorrowful-hearted,
    O gather us into Thine Heavenly home.
      We greet Thee, &c.

---

* From "Easter-tide," a Service of Song; also in "New and Old."

* No. XI.

Out of the Deep.

"*Forget those horrid stiles of death: see here*
Who died, and by His presence there
Imbalm'd the graue. See here Who rose, and so
Left hell infeebled, and the powers below
And death suppress'd. So that a child (no doubt)
May safely play w'th't now the sting's pluck'd out."
—Phineas Fletcher, 1640.

OUT of the deep there came
    From Hades, world unseen,
A Conqueror, Who there awhile had been:
    His triumph we proclaim.
      Our Paschal lay
      This joyous Day
Is, as the years roll on, for aye the same.

    Deep answereth to deep: †
    Jesu's unfathomed love
Adown did stoop from yon bright Heaven above
    To weep with them that weep,
      To dry all tears,
      To calm all fears,
And bid His people take their peaceful sleep.

---

* Published in "The Gospeller," A.D. 1892.

† "The deep of His mercies will answer to the deep of our miseries."—*Keble, on Psalm cxxx.*

May not their bodies cry *
To JESUS from the dust—
(For to His keeping we our dear ones trust)
While in the grave they lie,
Out of that deep
Wherein they sleep,
For joyful Resurrection with the just?

To Him must all things bow:
Death and the grave no more
Henceforth dare claim (their short-lived victory o'er),
Their dread dominion now.
Our ceaseless praise
We joy to raise
In Sion's Courts, as we perform our vow.

† No. XII.

Old Things and New.

"*Alleluia.*"

F newness is our song to-day,
For all things of new life are telling:
With Winter old things pass away,
As Spring once more asserts her sway,
And 'stablishes anew her dwelling.
Alleluia! Alleluia!

---

* "And may not the bodies of the faithful, buried in the dust, be said to cry out of the depths of the grave for a joyful resurrection, according to the promise and pattern of CHRIST, Who after three days came forth from the heart of the earth?"—*Bishop Horne.*

† Published in "Newbery House Magazine," A.D. 1892.

The joyous Day-spring from on high
  Again the gloom of night is chasing;
All Nature in bright garb arrayed
Hath new-born loveliness displayed,
  Dark days with sunshine now replacing.
                    Alleluia !

And e'en as when the LORD did shed
  His priceless blood for man's salvation,
And when He meekly bow'd His head,
As from the world His Spirit fled,
  Earth needs must mark her lamentation,
                    Alleluia !

So year by year, when Easter-tide
  All Nature's sympathy is claiming,
Earth needs must share the Church's joy—
True gladness, and with least alloy,
  While now her Risen LORD proclaiming.
                Alleluia ! Alleluia !

* No. XIII.

The Holy Women at the Sepulchre.

ON the eve before the Sabbath,
    Ere the setting of the sun,
  There were holy women sitting
    And beholding what was done,
In that garden where was lying
  One Whose wants were aye their care;
In their hearts still love must linger,
  Who nor toil, nor cost did spare.

---

* Published in "Newbery House Magazine," with music, A.D. 1891.

There awhile they were reposing
　In the Sabbath's sacred rest;—
Once again, its duties ended,
　Theirs must be an eager quest;
For, ere yet the sun had gilded
　With his early matin ray
That new tomb in Joseph's garden,
　They had ta'en their anxious way.

What strange vision there awaits them!
　Theirs what joy! and yet what awe!
As the glist'ning angels sitting
　In the empty tomb they saw.
O what wondrous salutation
　When the heavenly stranger said—
"Wherefore seek ye now the Living
　In the confines of the dead?"

Countless souls once more beholding,
　With the eye of faith, that scene,
Now recount the glorious vision
　By the holy women seen;
With great joy they hail the Victor
　Over death, and hell, and grave,
Who arose that Easter morning—
　LORD Almighty now to save.

* No. XIV.

The Smitten Shepherd.

"As a shepherd seeketh out his flock in a day that he is among his sheep that are scattered: so will I seek out My sheep, and will deliver them out of all places where they have been scattered in the cloudy and dark day."—EZEKIEL XXXIV. 12.

THE loving Shepherd smitten—
   Dark and cloudy was the day
When the scatter'd sheep did wander
   Each along his lonely way:—
But a brighter morn was dawning,
   When once more within the fold
The wand'rers shall be gather'd,†
   As their Shepherd had foretold.

That Shepherd was no hireling ‡
   Who would shrink in craven fear,
When He saw the wolf approaching,
   And the utmost danger near.
"Greater love than this hath no man," §
   For His precious life He gave
To save the sheep so helpless
   From the terrors of the grave.

---

* Published in "New and Old," A.D. 1891.

† "Then saith JESUS—'It is written I will smite the Shepherd, and the sheep of the flock shall be scattered abroad. But after I am risen again, I will go before you into Galilee.'"—*S. Matt.* xxvi. 32.

‡ S. John x. 12.   § S. John xv. 13.

Since that first Easter morning
  Joseph's empty tomb reveal'd,
And from Heav'n the mighty Angel
  Roll'd back the stone they seal'd,
From out so many places
  All the straying have been sought:
'Mid days all dark and cloudy
  Safely home the sheep were brought.

For JESUS goes before them,
  All the erring ones to guide;
He, the good and tender Shepherd,
  Bids them shelter at His side.
And throughout our life so changeful
  We can hear His gentle voice,
Who died, but now is risen,
  In Whose triumph we rejoice.*

† No. XV.

There is Gladness in the Air.

THERE is gladness in the air,
  All around and everywhere,
For the Spring so fresh and fair
    Comes again:
And with verdure clad anew,
'Neath a dome of cloudless blue,
Decks with garb of varied hue
    Hill and plain.

---

* 1 S. Peter i. 8.

† Published in "The Gospeller." Printed in the "Wesleyan General Hymnary for Special Services," &c.

With an endless beauty rife,
Newly quicken'd into life,
'Mid the world's discordant strife,
    Hear it say,
"Ev'ry Winter ushers Spring,
Each night's gloom the morn shall bring,
And its heaviness shall fling
    Far away."

See yon radiant sunlit bow,
With its many-tinted glow,
Springing from the earth below,
    Doth unfold
How the wrath of GOD is o'er,
How, like Sin and Death, no more
Shall the wasting floods outpour
    As of old.

"Easter triumph, Easter joy,"
Tell of bliss without alloy;
Life, no Death can e'er destroy,
    Has begun!
Hear again the welcome word,
Through successive ages heard,
CHRIST is risen! CHRIST the LORD!
    Lo! 'tis done.

*No. XVI.

To Emmaus.

THE struggle with sin and death was o'er,
    And a day had dawned full of joy and gladness;
But hearts there were still stricken and sore,
    Whose fond hopes were crush'd, and their lot was sadness.
Two lonesome souls, as they journey'd on,
    Were on scenes of the deepest gloom conversing,
For the staff on which they lean'd was gone,
    All their trust for deliverance subversing.

Lo! now came One Who would know their grief,
    And fain would soothe, with His merciful healing,
Their downcast spirits and bring relief—
    The wondrous scheme of Redemption revealing.
And soon their sad hearts within them burn,
    The Stranger disquieting doubts dispelling,
Their thoughts to the Written Word did turn,
    While their groundless fears His rebuke was quelling.

With them we journey in thought to-day,
    We sing of Emmaus, in Him confiding
Who comforts desponding souls by the way—
    Ever our Guide and our Guardian abiding.
"The LORD is risen" † our greeting be,
    While our fellow-pilgrims the salutation
With joy shall re-echo ceaselessly—
    "He is risen indeed," † Who is Salvation.

---

* Published in the "Penny Post," A.D. 1892.

† The Easter greeting of the Greek Church is, "The LORD is risen," and the response is, "He is risen indeed."

Ascension-tide Carols.

*No. I.

Carol we Joyfully.

CAROL we joyfully
    While we recall
    How, when His mission o'er,
    Crowning it all,
Jesus went up for us,
    Lifting His hands,
Blessings betokening
    Unto all lands.
        Carol we gratefully,
           Jesu, to Thee,
        For Thou didst "captive lead
           Captivity."

O'er us still lift Thine hands,
    Saviour, to bless;
Pierc'd with those marks of love,
    Our Righteousness.
Unto the throne of grace
    Through Thee we come:
Access Thou grantest us
    To Thy bright Home.
        Carol we, &c.

---

* From "Ascension-tide," a Service of Sacred Song, on S.P.C.K. Supplemental Catalogue, A.D. 1882.

For our infirmities
  Able to feel;
Sin's deep and deadly wounds
  Waiting to heal.
Gone to prepare for us
  Mansions on high,
Thither to follow Thee,
  And find Thee nigh.
    Carol we, &c.

* No. II.

God is Gone Up.

GOD is gone up—
  Right merrily the strain
  Once more we raise to echo on again!
From year to year,—roused by the prophet's call
The nations keep the glorious Festival.
    GOD is gone up. Hark! how the song
      Through Christendom doth ring!
    GOD is the King of all the earth;
      With strain of skill your praises sing.

GOD is gone up—
Who did to earth descend,
Who far above all Heavens doth ascend,
That "all things with His presence He may fill,"
And death and hell lead captive at His will.
    GOD is gone up, &c.

---

* Published in "The Church Musician."

GOD is gone up—
He o'er the heathen reigns
Exalted now—made perfect by His pains!
The LORD is high, upon His holy seat
He sitteth, all His foes beneath His feet.
   GOD is gone up, &c.

GOD is gone up—
The LORD with trumpet-sound—
Celestial Courts with joy resound:
Ere long th' Archangel's trump shall sound again
The JUDGE to herald, with His Angel train.
   GOD is gone up, &c.

* No. III.

"As Far as unto Bethany."

"Ye that to Heau'n direct your curious eyes,
And send your minds to walk the spacious skies,
See how the Maker to yourselues He brings,
Who sets His noble markes on meanest things;
And hauing man aboue the angels plac'd,
The lowly earth more than the Heau'n hath grac'd."
   —SIR JOHN BEAUMONT, 1582-1623.

" "S far as unto Bethany"
  The chosen ones were led,
 "Unto the Mount of Olivet"
  They journey'd with their Head:
   "Lo! I am alway with you,"
   Hear Him say,
   In Zion's holy city
   Ye must stay.

---

* Published in "New and Old."

'Twas at that self-same Bethany
  Where Martha served her LORD;
Where, at His feet, sat Mary once
  To hearken to His word.
    Was it for benediction
      JESUS came?
    Or hearts with holy rapture
      To inflame?

With joy—yet sorrow uppermost,
  Beheld that little band
Their fond and loving Master raise
  Each nail-imprinted hand:
    Hand now upraised in blessing
      As He rose;
    With fervid aspiration
      Each heart glows.

The angels on His natal day
  His advent did declare,
And angels for His dread return
  Bid sons of men prepare:
    With angels and archangels
      Now we raise
    To CHRIST the LORD ascended
      Songs of praise.

Harvest-tide Carols.

*No. I.

Brightly Breaks the Dawn of Day.

"He that soweth and he that reapeth shall rejoice together."

BRIGHTLY breaks the dawn of day,
    Calling forth an Autumn morn;
Reapers carol on their way
    To the fields of golden corn.
        Tra la la! I hear them singing;
        Tra la la! the air is ringing
            With their joyous melody.
        Tra la la! tra la la!
        Plenteous may the Harvest be.

Rouse ye, honest sons of toil,
    In the early morning's prime;
Rich shall be your labour's spoil
    In the gladsome Harvest-time.
        Tra la la! &c.

Yours it is to gather in
    Food for earth's vast family;
Yours the meed of praise to win—
    Honour to your labours be!
        Tra la la! &c.

---

* Published in "The Gospeller," A.D. 1889.

  And when fully-laden wains
   Home the last ripe loads shall bear,
  Reapers, then, to crown their pains
   Shall to Harvest-home repair.
    Tra la la! they shall be singing;
    Glad refrains shall then be ringing,
     All in joyful harmony :
      Tra la la! tra la la!
    Praise the Harvest's LORD will we.

* No. II.

Forth to the Waving Seas of Golden Grain.

" Seed time and harvest shall not cease."

FORTH to the waving seas of golden grain,
 The sturdy reapers hie at early morn,
The "staff of life" to gather once again,
 GOD'S yearly never-failing gift of corn.
GOD speed their work—GOD send them weather fair.
 His "the appointed weeks of Harvest-tide,"
The rustling sheaves proclaim His tender care,
 His faithful promise that shall aye abide.

His was the kindly warmth of summer sun,
 From Him the nurture of the nightly dew,
Their course, ordained by Him, the seasons run,
 From "out the earth He bringeth food" anew.
Mindful of men—unmindful can they be
 Of Him, Who op'neth wide His bounteous hand?
Who in His never-ending charity
 Vast multitudes doth feed through all the land.

---

* Published in " The Banner of Faith," and in Chope's Book of Carols.

* No. III.

O Come, Lift up your Eyes.

"Lift up your eyes and look on the fields, for they are white already to Harvest."

COME, "lift up your eyes, and look
    Upon the fields" now ripe once more,
O scan this page in nature's book,
    Outspread before us as of yore.
What various agencies conspire
    To gild with golden hue the land;
The sun looks forth with eye of fire,
    The rain—it falls on ev'ry hand.
    O come, "lift up your eyes and look
        Upon the fields" now ripe once more,
    O scan this page in nature's book,
        Outspread before us as of yore.

The light that o'er the teeming earth
    Breaks from the East, and, morn by morn,
It gives to countless blades their birth,
    To yield, ere long, full ears of corn.
O turn, and look on other fields
    Outspread before us—more sublime;
Think what their priceless Harvest yields,
    Souls from the Harvest-fields of time.
    O come, "lift up," &c.

---

* Published in "New and Old."

*No. IV.

Once More 'tis Harvest-tide.

*"You sun-burn'd sicklemen, of August weary,
Come hither from the furrow, and be merry."*
—"Tempest," Act 4, Scene 1.

NOW amid the hills and vales,
　　Along the smiling plains,
　In the stillness of the morn,
　　Are heard the cheery strains
Of each sturdy reaper band,
Far and wide throughout the land,
　　For once more 'tis Harvest-tide.

Hark! their joyous matin song!
　　Their carol by the way
Wakes the sportive echoes round;
　　Their merry roundelay
Seems to tell of earnest will
All their labours to fulfil:
　　For once more 'tis Harvest-tide.

May the bounteous Harvest LORD
　　Vouchsafe them cloudless skies,
And the welcome autumn breeze,
　　As each his sickle plies,
While they reap the fruitful field
And secure its golden yield:
　　For once more 'tis Harvest-tide.

---

* Published in "The Gospeller," A.D. 1890.

Then when crops are gather'd in,
   And all " are fill'd with good,"
From the mindful FATHER's Hand
   Who sends them yearly food,
They shall raise with joy the strain
   Of thanksgiving once again
     For the gifts of Harvest-tide.

* No. V.

Up, for the Glorious Autumn Sun.

"He that gathereth in summer is a wise son: but he that sleepeth in Harvest is a son that causeth shame."—PROV. X. 5.

UP, for the glorious Autumn sun
   The hills doth tinge
   With golden fringe:
The Harvest weeks are now begun!
   And earth once more
   Doth yield her store—
Ye sons of toil, uprouse ye!

While hedgerows yet are moist with dew,
   And early morn
   Just newly born
The face of nature doth renew,
   Ye may not waste
   The hours, but haste—
Ye sons of toil, uprouse ye!

---

* Published in " Banner of Faith."

Again outpour'd with bounteous hand,
    O'er hill and vale
    And shelter'd dale,
Rich gifts from Heav'n bedeck the land:
    To spoil each field
    Of golden yield,
Ye sons of toil, uprouse ye!

All hands must toil with right good will,
    Nor idly stray
    The live-long day:
With sheaves the garners ye must fill;
    Loud is the call
    On one and all—
Ye sons of toil, uprouse ye!

No recreant son in Harvest-tide
    May shun his part,
    Nor home depart,
Lest ill the "staff of life" betide—
    GOD'S yearly gift,
    Reward of thrift:
Then, sons of toil, uprouse ye!

✠

* No. VI.

Joy in Harvest.

"They joy before Thee according to the joy in harvest, and as men rejoice when they divide the spoil."—ISAIAH IX. 3.

WITH joy we sing of Harvest
    That crowns the waning year,
  When now once more its bounties
    On ev'ry side appear:
Adown the sloping hillside,
Along the fertile vale,
Amid the plains far-reaching,
GOD's yearly gift we hail.
    With joy we sing of Harvest
      That crowns the waning year,
    When now once more its bounties
      On ev'ry side appear.

† "The husbandman with patience
  The precious fruit of earth
Awaits, until receiving
  The rain" of priceless worth,
"The early rain and latter":
  When first he sows his seed,
And when the ears are swelling
  On hill and dale and mead.
    With joy we sing, &c.

Now eagerly to gather
  The fruit of all their toil,
Men sally forth right early
  The golden fields to spoil:

---

* Published in "The Gospeller," A.D. 1892.   † S. James v. 7.

No pains or labour sparing
  Their booty rich to store,
When homeward wains come laden,
  When toil at last is o'er.
    With joy we sing, &c.

Though great be men's rejoicing,
  As victors, to divide
The spoil of vanquish'd foemen—
  A hostile nation's pride:
Yet greater far in Harvest
  Their universal joy,
The reapers' bloodless conquest
  Achieved with least alloy.
    With joy we sing, &c.

* No. VII.

Welcome, Welcome, Harvest-tide.

"While the earth remaineth, seed-time and Harvest . . . shall not cease."—GENESIS VIII. 22.

WELCOME, welcome, Harvest-tide,
  With its golden treasure!
Wants of earth once more supplied
  In no stinted measure.
That promise sure, again fulfilled, we hail;
" Seed-time and Harvest-tide shall never fail."

---

* Published in "The Gospeller" and "Penny Post."

Welcome, needful pains and toil,
　　Willing hands supplying:
　　Vale and hill-side to despoil,
　　With each other vying,
For now that promise sure fulfilled we hail,
" Seed-time and Harvest-tide shall never fail."

　　Welcome aid we now receive
　　　From each friend and neighbour,
　　Grudging not from morn till eve
　　　To bestow his labour,
When now that promise sure fulfilled we hail,
" Seed-time and Harvest-tide shall never fail."

　　Welcome, too, the Harvest o'er,
　　　Meed of thankful praises!
　　For the garnered winter store
　　　Each his tribute raises
To Him, Whose word fulfilled His people hail,
For " Seed-time and the Harvest do not fail."

PART II.
Secular.

Odes.

No. I.
Ode on Spring-tide.

FROM "WEST-COUNTRY POETS."

"Rise up, and come away. For, lo, the Winter is past, the rain is over and gone; the flowers appear on the earth; the time of the singing of birds is come."—SONG OF SOLOMON ii. 11, 12.

YES, rise and come—mark how yon orb of day
From gloom of night is stealing hours away;
And how at eve, as if reluctantly,
Now slowly sinks beyond the western sea!
Come, leave awhile the haunts of carking care,
To quaff with calm delight the genial air:
To scent, 'mid murmurs of the balmy breeze,
Fair Nature's incense wafted from the trees.
Come, quit the busy mart, the dusky street,
Life's dull routine—to climb with nimble feet
Some lofty hilltop, or some woodland glade,
Whence to the 'raptured gaze is seen displayed
The rural landscape with fresh beauty rife,
Its lanes and hedgerows bursting into life.
The woods, awhile so leafless, now so bright
In vernal garb, or where in virgin white,
Clad in their countless blooms the trees appear,
Betok'ning fruit to crown the waning year;
See where, rejoicing in new life, the lambs
Frisk in a gleesome mood around their dams,
* Or where the colts career with frequent bound,
Circling the verdant meadows round and round.

---

* "Ludit et in pratis luxuriatque pecus."—*Ovid*, "*Fasti.*"

The finny tribe, "instinct with life," * are seen
Sporting amid the streams in silver sheen.
Deftly the feathered songsters twine each nest
For tender broods a refuge and a rest;
Flitting from spray to spray the woods among,
† From morn 'till eve pour forth their ceaseless song.
The cuckoo's well-known notes are heard once more,
Nor tire the ear though warbled o'er and o'er.
The gentle lark uprising, soars on high,
Trilling from tiny throat sweet minstrelsy;
Their roundelays the tuneful thrushes sing
The livelong day, to hail the approaching spring.
‡ "The beauteous season," in its fairest dress,
Appears again in new-born loveliness.
On earth, in air, and o'er the sunlit sea,
On mountain-top, or verdure-covered lea,
In woodland copse, with foliage crowned anew,
Where flow'rets spring in tints of endless hue,
On breezy down, or slope of sunny hill,
By stately-flowing stream, or silver rill,
In deep secluded dell, or widening plain,
Decked daintily in greenest garb again;
Above, below, around, afar, or near—
No longer trace is found of Winter drear.
All, all to eye and ear, with least alloy,
Bespeak fresh life, and whisper hope and joy:
While through her wide domain, in sweet accord,
§ Lo! Nature thus proclaims her risen LORD.

---

* "Instinct with life."—*Faber.*

† "Et tepidium volucres concentibus aëra mulcent."—*Ovid, "Fasti."* ‡ The French call Spring " La belle saison."

§ "And what is Spring after Winter but Nature speaking of the Resurrection of her LORD? It is the season when day is lengthening and mastering the night; light is overcoming darkness, and life springing out of apparent death, as in the returning presence of Him, Who is very Life, and very Light, and maketh all things new."—*Isaac Williams,* " *The Resurrection.*"

* **No. II.**

Jubilee Ode.

FOR THE 50TH ANNIVERSARY OF HER MAJESTY'S ACCESSION.

RING out ye bells, with blithesome peal, ring out!
On land and sea let British cheers a greeting shout!
Ye minstrels raise to-day your choicest strain,
And let it echo far and wide o'er hill and plain.
And when night's shades creep on and voices tire,
Light up on hill and tor the blazing beacon fire,
Yea, spread the joy, bid all the land rejoice
VICTORIA's Jubilee to greet with heart and voice.

Hail, worthy Scion, thou, of Brunswick's line!
For thee our strains we tune, our chaplets twine,
Upon our breasts the festal token † wear
To tell how England's Queen is cherish'd there:
And countless hearts for her GOD's blessing pray
On this her Fiftieth Accession Day.

Now bid the busy hum of labour cease,
Let weary sons of toil find brief release:
With good old English fare let rich men cheer
To-day the poor man's cottage far and near,
For on this morn a loyal Nation brings
Its glad Thanksgiving to the KING of kings.

And now a grateful people homage pay
To Royal worth, and heartfelt love display
The mem'ry of her lengthen'd reign shall dwell
In hearts that know to value her so well:
While in their universal joy is seen
How British subjects honour Britain's Queen.

---

* Printed in " Memorial Tributes."

† Her Majesty was pleased to express her wish that the rose— England's national emblem—should be worn as her flower token.

No. III.
Ode on the Consecration of Truro Cathedral.

RESPECTFULLY INSCRIBED TO THE RIGHT REV. GEO. HOWARD,
LORD BISHOP OF TRURO.

"*Sacerdos:* "Ανω σχῶμεν τὰς καρδίας.* *Populus:* "Εχομεν πρὸς τὸν Κύριον."—LITURGY OF CÆSAREA.

IT is the Year of Jubilee
Of England's joy in England's Queen,
And many a noble monument,
To tell how great that joy has been,
Her people for posterity
Have rear'd, with lavish treasure spent:
And, mindful whence all blessings flow,
Nunc exultemus Domino.

It is the Day of Jubilee,
And England's Prince—whom GOD preserve!—
To our far West has come once more,
The cause of England's Church to serve,
The witness of her joy to be;
Lis Escop † stablish'd as of yore
Shall old Cornubia's people see.
Cantemus, fratres, hodiè.

Devonia hails Thy Jubilee,
United long—not sunder'd now;
One faith, one baptism, one LORD,
With fervent zeal her sons avow,

---

* "Cyprian, in the third century, attested the use of the form, 'Lift up your hearts,' and its response, in the Liturgy of Africa. Certainly used in the English Liturgy ever since A.D. 595."— *Palmer's* "*Origines Liturgicæ.*"

† Old Cornish for "Bishop's house."

Fresh tokens of His grace we see
While holding fast His sacred Word;
And now, on this auspicious day,
Oremus pro ecclesiâ.

Be this thy time of Jubilee,
Sound forth thy call with trumpet tone,
From out thy Mother-Church's fane,
Cornubia, yearning for thine own
To heal their broken unity,
And gather in Thy sons again:
Let not our * *Sursum corda* cease,
" *Unus et omnes* " †—*nostra spes!*

Festival of All Saints, A.D. 1887.

No. IV.
Ode on The Beautiful.

"He hath made everything beautiful in his time."—ECCLES. iii. 11.

ASK not where is Beauty's dwelling,
   Ask not what are Beauty's laws,
   All around is ever telling
     Of the First, the One great Cause!
Hearts untutor'd find its trace,
Eyes unpractised see its place—
Earth, and Ocean spreading far,
Beauty's wide dominions are.

---

* See footnote on preceding page.
† Ancient Cornish motto.

Beauty reigns in every season,
   And in countless shapes it lives,
Why enquire of human reason
   What is that which Beauty gives?
Eyes so blind and dim may be,
Hearts so dull as ne'er to see
All the beautiful and bright
Plainly traced to keener sight.

Gaze o'er yon expanse of Ocean,
   Watch it in its "countless smile"!*
Sparkling now in ceaseless motion,
   Sinking into calm awhile,
Or, when stirr'd in deep unrest,
Crown'd with many a snow-white crest—
Emblem of His Majesty
Dwelling in Eternity.

In returning Spring it meets thee
   With its sights and sounds so gay,
'Neath the Summer sunshine greets thee
   E'en throughout the live-long day:
To the waning Autumn cleaves
As it paints the falling leaves:
What though winter be its tomb,
Still it lingers in the gloom.

In the brightly-flowing streamlet
   As it threads its silvery way,
In the softly-tinted leaflet
   Hanging from each graceful spray,
In earth's garb of grassy green
Beauty's presence may be seen,
In the cornfield's golden hue,
And in Heaven's arch of blue,

---

* "κυμάτων ἀνήριθμον γέλασμα."—*Æsch: Prom.*

Infancy its source revealing,
   Childhood marks its secret growth,
To all eyes and hearts appealing
   In the comely form of youth;
Who is he that hath not seen
Beauty in fair maiden's mien?
Who but owns its potent charm
In the lovely female form?

Beauty still must ever linger
   In our sin-polluted earth,
Ruin, with despoiling finger,
   May not check its constant birth.
Whence the Beautiful? and why?
   Source and reason would'st thou know?
Nature answers silently *—
   † "Heavenly Wisdom made it so."

---

* " There is neither speech nor language, but their voices are heard among them."—*Psalm xix.* 3.

† " O LORD, how manifold are Thy works! in wisdom Thou hast made them all: the earth is full of Thy riches. So is the great and wide Sea also."—*Psalm civ.* 24, 25.

Songs.

*No. I.

When shall the Din of Warfare Cease?

WHEN shall the din of warfare cease—
   Its harvests of death be o'er?
When shall the nations find release,
   And earth be oppress'd no more?
When shall the lust of conquest dire
   Human blood no longer shed,
And sword and fire with relentless ire
   Never more pile up the dead?

When shall ambition cease to sway
   The hearts of earth's mighty kings?
When will men loathe the ghastly fray
   The discord of nations brings?
Ah! when shall thoughts of widows' wail,
   Or fast-flowing orphans' tears
Fierce warriors turn from their purpose stern
   And soothe gentle woman's fears?

Enough of slaughter—ruthless woe!
   Enough of dying men's moans—
Those dismal cries borne from the plain,
   And those deep, those heart-wrung groans!
Bid men their blood-stain'd banners furl
   Seek to stay the foemen's tread,
Restrain the hands of their warlike bands
   Filling peaceful souls with dread.

---

* Adapted to music by Klitz.

Pray God to speed the happy day
  When the din of war shall cease,
From dire alarms and clash of arms
  May the world soon find release!
When swords to ploughshares men shall beat
  Grim harvests of death be o'er
And men inclined to a holier mind
  Hateful war shall learn no more.

* No. II.

Return, Sweet Peace.

A SONG FOR THE TIMES.

RETURN, sweet peace, for thee we sigh—
  O tarry thou no more;
Ah, when shall we behold thee nigh?
  Speed Thou from shore to shore.
Hush'd be the war trump's echoing blast—
  The call to slaughter dire,
And thund'ring cannon flashing fast
  With devastating fire.
    Return, sweet peace, &c.

Say, what is glory—what is fame
  In utmost peril sought?
A fleeting good—an empty name,
  Alas! so dearly bought.

---

* Written during the Crimean War, and sung on many successive nights in the Agricultural Hall, Islington. Set to music by Alfred B. Burrington, Esq.

Grim carnage marks the deadly fray
  Ambition's craving brings ;
Death's angel broods o'er honour's way,
  Destruction on his wings.
    Return, sweet peace, &c.

Swift o'er the surging billows' foam
  Be weary sailors borne!
And speedy to his distant home
  The soldier's lov'd return!
For hearts are sad and homes are drear
  Amid the war's alarms;
Sweet peace return, now doubly dear,
  Since we have lost thy charms.
    Return, sweet peace, &c.

No. III.
Side by Side and Hand in Hand.

SIDE by side and hand in hand
  We will take our way together:
Two and two life's pilgrim band
  Journey on through wind and weather.
Troth for troth, in woe or weal,
  In the sacred courts when plighted:
Lip with lip still be the seal,
  Lest fond earthly hopes be blighted.

Joy in joy we share anew
  While our summer days are gliding:
Grief meets grief while passing through
  Winter's gloom, its storms abiding.

Each to each we duties owe,
  Petty grievances we smother,
Heart to heart, as on we go,
  Shall respond the one to other.

Eye to eye be ours to see—
  Will with will together blended,
Step with step shall measur'd be
  Till our pilgrimage be ended.
Side by side and hand in hand,
  Nothing shall our compact sever
When we reach the far-off strand
  No more partings shall be ever.

No. IV.
A Christmas Song.

ADAPTED TO KUCKEN'S "DES BERGMAUN'S LIED."

OH, blithe and blest is Christmas-tide,
    Whene'er its season comes
  We hail it ever with delight,
  For hearts are light and eyes are bright
    In England's happy homes;
We'll use its harmless mirth aright,
We'll gather all, both great and small,
    In social ring,
And once a year our carols clear
    Right lustily we'll sing.

Though bleak and chill the wintry wind,
  And frost be hard and keen,
We'll circle closely round the fire,
Of music's strains we shall not tire,
  We love them well I ween,

Both young and old, and son and sire,
Our part and voice we all rejoice
    Again to bring,
And once a year our carols clear
    Right lustily we'll sing.

With hearts elate, good friends, 'tis meet
    Our cheerful songs should rise,
For at this season long ago
Peace and goodwill mankind did know,
    First chanted in the skies,
And shall be echoed here below;
With joyous lays and hymns of praise
    The world shall ring;
And every year, its carols clear
    Right lustily shall sing.

* No. V.

Christmas Vocal Gavotte.

HOME once more! to the dear old home,
    Hark! those rollicking boys are come!
Where there's bustle and jest and noise,
    There, be sure, are those dread-nought boys.
"Boys will be boys" the old folks say,
They, too, were boys and girls one day:
And they say in France of each lad and lass,
"Oui, mais il faut que la jeunesse se passe."
(Yes, but youthful days one has need to pass.)

---

* Set to music by A. H. Brown.

Home once more! to the dear old home,
Hark! those frolicsome girls are come!
'Twixt girls and boys with modern views
I don't think there's a pin to choose:
At Christmas, too, there's bound to be
A gush of frolic, fun, and glee.
    For they say in France, &c.

Pater and mater, here we are,
Tasks and books we have banish'd far;
We get, like turkeys, lots of cram,
Not for Christmas but stiff exam.:
No wonder, then, when term is o'er,
That your young hopefuls don't want more.
    For they say in France, &c.

We've counted days for some time past,
Father Christmas has come at last,
All blithe and merry won't we be
Keeping the old Festivity?
And when old Janus* shall appear
We'll wish all friends "A happy New Year."
For they say in France of each lad and lass,
" Oui, mais il faut que la jeunesse se passe."

---

   * The old heathen god, hence the name of January.

*No. VI.

Bells on New-Year's Eve.

HARK! 'mid the stillness of the night
    Sweet sounds salute the ear:
Though heard in gloom they sing of light,
Their notes are joyous, clear, and bright;
Theirs is a strain of deep delight,—
    They greet the new-born year!

Yet sad enough to many hearts
    The merry New-Year's peal:
No solace sweet that strain imparts
To selfish churls; true joy departs
From such as these,—by other arts
    They joy, who *true* joy feel.

Ay, glad to all who start anew
    On life's unceasing round:
Who, with the distant goal in view,
The onward, upward, path pursue:
Who shun false joys to gain the true,
    Right glad to these the sound.

Ring on, ring on, ye joyous bells,
    In gladsome cadence clear:
Of fresh resolves your music tells,
As on the midnight air it swells,
Your chime the short-lived gloom dispels—
    Ye greet the glad New Year.

---

* Published in "Church Bells" of December 30th, 1887.

Church Defence Songs.

No. I.
The City of our Solemnities.

OUR grand old Church of England,
   Long years have seen it stand—
Of faith the lasting bulwark,
   The glory of our land:
All dangers yet surviving,
   As founded on a rock,
The fury of the tempest,
   The foeman's ruthless shock.

But see! the storm-clouds gather,
   The surging waters roar,
Our stronghold is beleaguer'd,
   Foes thunder at our door:
Then, brothers, all uprouse ye,
   The Nation's Church defend,
No carnal weapons wielding,
   In lawful strife contend.

This is no time for slumber,
   Each man must take his post,
And rally round his banner
   To face a well-trained host:
Our Zion's walls they threaten
   And compass them around,
Hark, how the cry increases—
   "Down with them to the ground."

> For righteous cause contend we,
>   Vast issues are at stake,
> Those trusts our sires bequeath'd us
>   We guard for children's sake,
> May Church and State united
>   Still be, as they have been—
> Long live that godly union,
>   GOD save our Church and Queen!

A.D. 1885.

* No. II.

The Old Village Church of our Fathers.

"Look upon Zion, the city of our solemnities; thine eyes shall see Jerusalem a quiet habitation, a tabernacle that shall not be taken down; not one of the stones thereof shall ever be removed, neither shall any of the cords thereof be broken."—ISAIAH XXXIII. 20.

> THE old village Church of our fathers!
>   All its stones have grown grey with years,
> And the record of by-gone ages
>   On the stately enclosure appears.
> Fond mem'ries have cluster'd around it
>   From earliest days until now,
> Serenely it stands, like some grandsire—
>   The time-furrows writ on his brow.

---

* Published by Church Defence Institution. Set to music by E. H. Thorne.

'Twas here many past generations
 Of our ancestors met to pray—
Sire, son, gentle maiden, and matron,
 Rich, poor, young and old came to pay
Their homage and kneel at yon altar
 When bells would invite to these walls.
To-day, still, the same "angel-music" *
 To matins and evensong calls.

But the "poor man's palace" no longer
 Some have said the old Church shall be:
With impious hands they would seize it
 Who, in strange animosity,
Having evil will 'gainst our Zion,
 Would compass her fall, if they dared—
But the voice of indignant England
 Demands that her fanes shall be spared.

Then close up your ranks, Brother Churchmen,
 While shoulder to shoulder ye stand;
Stay the spoiler from dire desecration
 Of Churches—the pride of your land.
On might of the Mighty One leaning,
 Our loins let us gird for the fight:
Our aim be—"Defence not Defiance,"
 Our watchword—"FOR GOD AND THE RIGHT."

---

* "Think when the bells do chime
'Tis angels' music."—*Geo. Herbert.*

No. III.

To Arms! To Arms!

ADAPTED TO SIR J. BARNBY'S TUNE ("HYMNARY," 640),
"WE MARCH, WE MARCH TO VICTORY."

"The weapons of our warfare are not carnal, but mighty through God."

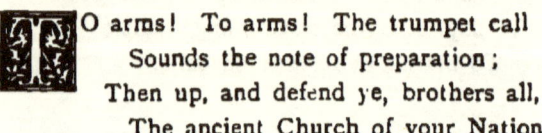O arms! To arms! The trumpet call
    Sounds the note of preparation;
Then up, and defend ye, brothers all,
    The ancient Church of your Nation.

Yet with carnal weapons ye must not fight,
    When foes of your Zion surround you,
But bravely unite,—to strive for the right,
    With your trusty armour around you.
        To arms, &c.

In no strength of his own the Christian boasts,
    Yet the weapons he wields are mighty,
For the Captain He serves is the LORD OF HOSTS,
    And his "Rock of Defence"—the ALMIGHTY.
        To arms, &c.

With the Sword of the SPIRIT in his hands,
    In his Master's Name he must wield it,
Nor for Zion fear from the hostile bands
    If the great GOD of battles shield it.
        To arms, &c.

Don we then the "breast-plate of Righteousness,"
    The pure Gospel of peace adorning:
With "the shield of faith" when the foemen press,
    When, in danger, the trump gives warning.
        To arms, &c.

When in trustful faith GOD'S own people pray,
    Then "He knappeth the spear in sunder,"
"He breaketh the bow" in the deadly fray
    As of old, with His voice of thunder.
        To arms, &c.

"Go round our lov'd Zion and count her towers,"
    Lo! her bulwarks are strong before us!
Neither crafts, nor assaults, nor evil powers
    Shall prevail, if His arm be o'er us.
        To arms, &c.

Then the LORD GOD of Jacob will we take
    As our GOD for ever and ever,
He will watch o'er His Church for JESU'S sake
    Which nought from His keeping shall sever.
        To arms, &c.

Vocal Trios.

*No. I.
Welcome to the Spring.

SING welcome to the Spring-time,
    The bright, the joyous Spring,
In strains of liveliest measure
    Your hearty welcome bring;
All nature, now rejoicing,
    Puts on her fairest dress,
From wintry gloom reviving
    To new-born loveliness.

The streamlet in its freedom
    From winter's icy chain
Leaps forth as if in gladness
    To course along the plain;
The playful lambs are frisking
    And sporting in the mead,
The neighing colt is bounding,
    Exulting in his speed.

The buds with life are bursting
    In light and sombre green,
The trees, with snow-white blossoms,
    Are deck'd in virgin sheen;
The balmy breeze is laden
    With perfum'd breath of flowers,
The feather'd songsters warble
    Amid the verdant bow'rs.

---

* Published, with music, in Pitman's "Vocal Trios."

*No. II.
Wild Flowers.
ADAPTED TO MUSIC BY MOZART.

A DOWN the dells, on breezy hills,
  'Mid hedgerows green, on sunny slope
By streamlet's bank or sparkling rills,
  Your blooms in rich profusion ope;
Your perfume sweet the breezes bear,
Your bright gems meet us everywhere.

Ye deck the mossy woodland glade
  With tints so beautiful and bright,
At endless graceful forms display'd
  We gaze with wonder and delight,
And trace while we wild flow'rets twine
  The tokens of a Hand Divine.

†No. III.
Lullaby.
ADAPTED TO MUSIC BY SIR H. BISHOP.

SLEEP, fairest lady, the day's declining,
  The star of eve will soon be shining;
O may our dulcet strains delight thee,
And thus to soft repose invite thee.
    May slumber sweet
      Thine eyelids steep,
    Lull'd by our song,
      "Sweet sleep"—"sweet sleep."
    Bright be thy dreams
      Till morning light,
    Calm be thy rest,
      "Good night,"—"good night."

---
*Published by Pitman, in "Vocal Trios."   †Published by Pitman.

*No. IV.

Our Rural Holiday.

ADAPTED TO MUSIC BY DUSSEK.

WITH hopes so bright in merriest mood
   We join our festive meeting:
We quaff the breath of early morn,
   From dusky streets retreating.
     To sylvan scenes we hie us,
     On rural pleasures bent:
     The fields and woods supply us
       With joy to our heart's content.

The hedgerows, deck'd in holiday garb,
   Their fairest tints revealing,
Shall court the gaze and charm the eye,
   To beauty's sense appealing.
     The drooping ferns are bending
     O'er brook and silver stream,
     The sweet wild flowers are blending
       Their bright blooms where they gleam.

With blithesome music's happiest notes
   The echoes shall be ringing;
Repeating o'er the glad refrain
   Our tuneful band keep singing.
     While each his tribute raises
     In strains he loves right well,
     We gladly chant the praises
       Of grove and glade and dell.

---

* Published by Pitman.

* No. V.
The Sailor's Welcome Home from Sea.

ADAPTED TO MUSIC BY SIR H. BISHOP.

  LOOK forth! Look forth! A sail in sight
   To greet our weary, watchful eyes,
   We gaze with rapture and delight,
   A thrill of joy yon bark supplies.
Our prayers are heard, our hopes with joy are crown'd,
And now let mirthful glee with all abound:
   We'll shout and sing right merrily
   The sailor's welcome home from sea.

   They come! They come! All peril past,
   Storm-toss'd, yet safe at home at last,
   Safe from the dangers of the deep,
   Where mighty tempests round them sweep.
Oft when we heard the night-wind fiercely howl,
Or saw in murky skies an angry scowl,
   We fondly thought how heartily
   We'll sing the welcome home from sea.

   And now no more of dismal gloom,
   For nought but joy we now find room,
   As friends long absent reached the strand
   We clasp each honest, horny hand.
We'll not forget our meed of grateful praise
To Him, Who rules the raging sea, to raise,
   And then our cheerful song shall be
   The sailor's welcome home from sea.

---

* Published, with music, in Pitman's "Handbook of Vocal Trios."

Part Songs.

*No. I.

The Watch on the Rhine.

ADAPTED TO THE MUSIC OF THE GERMAN SONG.

THE war-trump echoes far and wide,
And calls to arms from side to side,
Along thy banks, my own lov'd Rhine,
Our warriors' burnish'd helmets shine—
   Thou land of Patriots still art mine,
   Roll on in peace, thou deep blue Rhine.

In serried ranks our youth shall stand
Defending our dear Fatherland;
Our noble river flowing wide
Rolls yet no dark or blood-stain'd tide.
   Thou land of Patriots, &c.

In pious love we guard Thy stream
Where hamlets smile and castles gleam,
Thy slopes bedeck'd with purple vine,
So fam'd in song, our own lov'd Rhine.
   Thou land of Patriots, &c.

Dear Rhine-land, may no rude hand mar
Thy beauty 'mid the din of war,
Thy sons, inspir'd with loyal love,
For thee the best of bulwarks prove.
   Thou land of Patriots, &c.

---

* Published, with music, in "The Part Singer."

* No. II.

The Sentinel's Dream.

HE sentinel his lone watch keeps
The while each weary comrade sleeps;
Tho' dark the gloom, he dreams of light—
While mem'ry paints her visions bright.

And in the long and lonesome hours,
In thought he visits home's sweet bow'rs,
To his mind's eye he sees expand
The scenes of his dear Fatherland.

And present in those watchful dreams
One witching form there ever seems,
To greet him with a welcome smile,
And thus his tedious hours beguile.

At duty's call she bade him go—
No recreant he to face the foe,
Yet fervent now her prayers for peace,—
From war his heart would hail release.

---

* Published, with music, in "The Part Singer."

* No. III.

Early Violets in Epiphany-tide.

LITTLE nurslings of the Winter,
    Of a season bleak and drear,
    Putting forth your modest petals
        Ere more gaudy blooms appear:—
He Who ting'd your simple flow'ret
    With its dye of regal blue,
He Who breath'd on you sweet perfume,
    Teaches parables by you.

What if 'neath the chilly snow-drift
    And amid the frost and cold,
Scarcely visited by sunshine,
    Ye do ope your eye of gold:—
What if 'mid the dripping bowers,
    And the sighing of the wind,
Ye do bloom in lonely places,
    And we there your fragrance find;

Ye are like the days of Childhood
    Of our meek and gentle LORD,
His—Who did in scenes so homely,
    Such a "savour sweet" afford,
Though in humble paths of duty,
    Seen by few, He daily trod,
Yet around Him breath'd an odour,
    It was redolent of GOD.

---

* Set to music by A. B. Burrington. First printed in "Church of England Temperance Magazine," A.D. 1870.

He it was, Who on the flowers,
  Did those words of wisdom preach,
He it is, Who still creates them
  Those abiding truths to teach.
Then take heart, e'en if but lowly
  In this life thy lot may be:
Let its fragrance gladden others
  In all meek simplicity.

*No. IV.

Opera Chorus.

ADAPTED TO THE PRAYER IN MOSE IN EGITTO.

LORD of all creation,
  Supreme o'er every nation,
  In lowly adoration
    We bend before Thy throne;
  Hear Thou our invocation,
    Receive us as Thine Own.

From all that would oppress us,
From ills that might distress us,
O shield us, LORD, and bless us
  In basket and in store;
Then with Thy love possess us,
  O FATHER, evermore.

We need Thine help and healing,
We crave Thy gracious dealing,
To us Thy love revealing,
  Our Guide and Guardian be;
O hear us while appealing
  For mercy, LORD, to Thee.

---

* Published, with music, in "The Part Singer."

Songs of Welcome and Greeting.

*No. I.

Song of Welcome

To their Graces the Duke and Duchess of Northumberland, on the Occasion of their Visit to Launceston, July 28th, a.d. 1857.

    LOUDLY Dunheved's sons should sing,
      Proudly their strain of welcome bring,
      While our old walls are echoing
        The glad and hearty song!
    The Sire of Percy's House we see
    And noble Grosvenor's "fair ladye"
    Are come our honour'd guests to be,
      The joyous strain prolong!
        Loudly Dunheved's sons should sing,
        Proudly their strain of welcome bring,
        While our old walls are echoing
        The glad and hearty song!

    Let our united company
    With hearts so light and strains so high,
    With notes of blithesome melody,
      Sing "Welcome to our Town!"
    Long may the Sires of Percy's line
    In deeds of love and virtue shine!
    May blessings from above combine
      Their noble race to crown!
        Loudly Dunheved's sons, &c.

---

* Sung in the Castle Green.

No. II.

Song of Greeting

FROM THE LAUNCESTON VOLUNTEERS TO THEIR COMPANIONS
IN ARMS, ON THE OCCASION OF THE BATTALION
DRILL, JULY 23RD, A.D. 1861.

AIR—"*March in Norma.*"

FROM old Dunheved's Castle wall
   Is heard afar th' "Assembly's" call,
   And hark the drum! for comrades come
     To join our ranks to-day.
Then haste with a friendly greeting
When with kindred spirits meeting,
For our hearts with pride are beating
   All honour thus to pay.
      And our heartiest music bring we,
      And the song of welcome sing we,
      The joyous strain we'll raise again
        On this our gala day.

Tho' stern and warlike be our guise,
Grim war is odious in our eyes;
We take up arms lest war's alarms
   Should rouse our native land.
On our cause we've firm reliance,
For "DEFENCE AND NOT DEFIANCE"
Has cemented our alliance
   And bids us watching stand.
      Then a song of welcome bring we,
      And in hearty chorus sing we,
      Yes, raise again the joyous strain,
        And grasp each friendly hand.

Whilst England bids us duteous be
We'll keep old Cornwall's Unity,
We'll rally all at duty's call
　Where honour bids us stay:
Tho' no danger yet has tried us
Let no discord e'er divide us,
Lest the foeman should deride us
　Confounded in the fray.
　　Now our heartiest music bring we,
　　And the song of welcome sing we,
　　The joyous strain we'll raise again
　　　On this our gala day.

No. III.

Song of Welcome

To the Most Honourable the Marquis of Salisbury,
England's Prime Minister.*

*Adapted to Bellini's Chorus ("Suoni la tromba"),
from "I Puritani."*

ROUSE ye, Devonia's sons, to-day,
　　Right worthy is the call!
　Comrades, upraise the tuneful lay,
　　A strain for one and all,
　As now together banding,
　Shoulder to shoulder standing,
　A noble cause inspires us,
　With ardent zeal it fires us,
Rouse ye, Devonia's sons, to-day,
　　Right worthy is the call!

---

*Sung on the occasion of his visit to the City of Exeter, January 19th, A.D. 1892, at a gathering of 10,000 people, and repeated on the night after.

Proudly each loyal denizen
  Unites with heart and hand,
And joins Devonia's husbandmen,
  A tried and trusty band,
In this our joyous meeting,
Old England's Premier greeting,
Of Cecil's house true scion,
One whom our hearts rely on.
Rouse ye, Devonia's sons, to-day,
  Right worthy is the call!

Guardian is he of Britain's fame,
  'Gainst ev'ry hostile power,
Upholding firmly her great name
  In peril's darkest hour :
Peace for our land procuring,
With honour, peace enduring;
A helmsman safe to guide us,
When stormy days betide us.
Rouse ye, Devonia's sons, to-day,
  Right worthy is the call!

Brothers, your timely aid prepare,
  Make strong your leader's hands,
Under our Premier's fost'ring care,
  Entire this Empire stands;
Of Church and State Protector,
Of laws the safe Director—
Then heartiest welcome bring we,
And heartfelt strains now sing we,
Devonia's sons respond to-day,
  For worthy is the call!
Huzza! Huzza! Huzza!
  Make strong your Leader's hands;
Huzza! Huzza! Huzza!
  Entire this Empire stands!

School Songs.

*No. I.

Breaking up for the Christmas Holidays

COME, schoolmates, let us jovial be:
    This is our festal day!
From toil and task we rest awhile,
Set free from book-lore:—Come, beguile
The hours with mirth in schoolboy style,
    And use them while we may.

Nor friends, nor masters, longer chide
    The weary wayward boy;
For fun and frolic now allied,
No notes of discord shall divide
Our merry hearts, but side by side
    We'll welcome Christmas joy.

It is but fair when work is o'er,
    Our well-earn'd rest should come;
We pause,—and then return once more
To toil more bravely than before,
With life and health—a fresh full store
    Drawn from the dear old home.

Three cheers, my lads, for hearths and homes,
    Three jolly British cheers.
Hurrah! for Christmas comes again!
Hurrah! for his time-honoured reign!
Hurrah! for all his jocund train!
    Now for your hearty cheers.
Hip! hip! hurrah! Hip! hip! hurrah!

---

* The music by Rev. J. B. Dykes, Mus. Doc. Written for the boys of the Launceston Grammar School.

*No. II.
In Palmy Days of Ancient Rome.

"*Dent operam consules, ne quid detrimenti respublica capiat.*"
—CÆSAR.

IN palmy days of ancient Rome,
    When hearts were brave and wills were strong,
  In order that no ill might come
    To vex the State or do it wrong,
They bade the consuls their " endeavour do."
So, boys, to School and selves let us be true.
    Dabimus operam " unus et omnes," †
      Ut semper floreat Schola Grammatica
        Cornubiensis. ‡

With pride we turn to days gone by,
  To records in the scroll of fame,
Writ of old Cornwall's ancestry,
  Of men who gain'd an honor'd name.
Schoolmates, let us be up and doing now,
This age with goodly names let us endow.
    Dabimus operam, &c.

In our old scutcheon we can see,
  Emblazon'd by the limner's skill,
A vessel sailing o'er the sea,
  Right onward, ever onward still.
Be this our motto, boys, "On, ever on,
Until the port be reached, the goal be won."
    Dabimus operam, &c.

---

* Written for the Truro Grammar School, by request of Rev. T. F. Maddrell, Head Master. The music by M. J. Monk, Mus. Doc.

† The ancient Cornish motto—" One and all."

‡ Translation—" We will, one and all, do our endeavour that the Cornish Grammar School may ever flourish."

Or by example would we learn
  What marvels earnest hearts can do,
To Truro's minster let us turn,
  And, as yon stately pile we view,
The lesson aye the school-boy's heart shall cheer
To work with right goodwill and persevere.
     Dabimus operam, &c.

✠

The Life=boats of the Church.

"Surely in the floods of great waters they shall not come nigh unto him."—PSALM XXXII. 6.

WITH fearless hearts and true the Church's life-boats man,
   To seek and save the perishing. For such the plan
The Heav'nly Master left her, when before His view
There rose the wrecks of ages! Therefore, dare and do.
Haste ye, launch forth, fear not, like Him be calm and brave
Amid the storms of life. Haste, rescue from the grave
And gate of death, from out the whelming floods of sin
Those souls, those priceless souls that Master died to win.
The awful thunder rolls—the lightning clears the sky—
Signs of GOD's wrath, and His offended Majesty:
Yet would He have the life-boats launch'd ere all be o'er,
And souls He strove to save shall sink, to rise no more.
Then haste ye, tell the perishing that help is near—
Those panic-stricken guilty souls o'erwhelmed with fear,
Tell them the LORD would have each soul salvation see
And safely reach the haven, where they fain would be.

✠

Translations and Adaptations from the French.

No. I.
Come ye to Him.

SACRED SONG,
Founded on the French of Victor Hugo.

"*Vous qui pleurez,—venez à ce Dieu,—car Il pleure.
Vous qui souffrez—venez à Lui,—car Il guérit.
Vous qui tremblez—venez à Lui,—car Il sourit.
Vous qui passez—venez à Lui—car Il demeure.*"

COME all, who bitter tears do shed in secret,
   Whose cup of woe is full e'en to the brim,
   Learn ye from One Who wept, calm resignation,
              Come ye to Him.

Come all, who throes of pain and anguish suffer,
   Ye can to Him those bitter pangs reveal,
   For pangs unspeakable were His endurance—
              Who skills to heal.

Come all, in penitence, whose spirits tremble,
   His smile is peace:—His words of pardon hear—
   "I will in no wise cast out him that cometh"—
              Why should ye fear?

Come all, who from this changeful world are passing
   When "flesh and heart shall fail," and eyes grow dim,
   Stay ye your souls on Him that changeth never,
              Abide in Him.

*No. II.

Confiance.

FROM THE FRENCH (AU DELA), BY ALICE DE CHAMBRIER. ‡

I tu sens vaciller ta foi
    Devant la tempête hagarde,
        Calme-toi, †
        Dieu te garde.

Si, d'après la commune loi,
Dans le néant tombe chaque heure,
    Calme-toi,
    Dieu demeure.

Si ton cœur est rempli d'émoi
Si le désespoir t'environne,
    Calme-toi,
    Dieu pardonne.

Si la mort te comble d'effroi,
Si tu crains l'ombre où l'on sommeille,
    Calme-toi,
    Dieu réveille.

---

* Printed by permission of Mons. Philippe Godet.

† "Be still, and know that I am GOD."—*Psalm xlvi.* 10.

‡ This gifted young writer fell asleep at xxi. years of age. Mons. Godet, who edited her work, says, "Le mot de sa destinée était *au delà !*"

No. II.

Trustfulness.

F thou perceive thy soul to fill
   With doubt, when now the storm is high
      Be still,†
     For GOD is nigh.

If Time its destiny fulfil,
And into nought each swift hour glides,
      Be still,
     For GOD abides.

If blank despair thy bosom chill,
While Hope within thee scarcely lives,
      Be still,
     For GOD forgives.

If dread of death thy spirit thrill—
Or gloom where mortals slumber take,
      Be still,
     God will thee wake.

---

† See footnote opposite.

* No. III.

L'Automne.

PAR MDLLE. A. DE CHAMBRIER.

'AUTOMNE nous arrive, et la Nature entière
Voyant, sombre et muet, son tombeau se rouvrir,
Comprend qu'elle est tout près de son heure dernière
El, le cœur désolé, se prépare à mourir.

Mais si d'après nos lois il faut qu'elle succombe,
Elle ne dira pas qu'elle se sent faiblir
El, radieuse, un jour descendra dans la tombe,
Sans que nos yeux aient vu son visage pâlir.

Car toute la Nature, en sa splendeur est femme,
Elle vent être belle à l'heure de la mort,
Elle vent emparer les regrets de notre âme,
Elle vent qu'ici bas nous pleurions sur sont sort.

C'est pourquoi, lorsque vient languissante l'automne,
Elle met un manteau tissé de pourpre et d'or
Et pour sa tête une triple couronne,
Dont les feux rayonnants le grandissent encor.

Sa robe de topaze étincelle, émaillée
De mille diamants aussi purs que les pleurs,
Et de ses blanches mains tristement effeuillées
On voit se détacher des corolles de fleurs.

---

* Printed by permission of Mons. Philippe Godet.

No. III.

Autumn.

TRANSLATED FROM THE FRENCH OF MDLLE. ALICE DE
CHAMBRIER.

O! Autumn comes, and in its speechless gloom,
All Nature sees expand once more her tomb:
Perceiving, as she does, her last hour nigh,
With heart disconsolate, prepares to die.

Yet, if it be decreed she needs must fail,
No sense of weakness shall with her prevail:
Into that tomb she will descend one day—
No pallor on that face that fades away.

For Nature, in her glory, Woman is—
E'en fading charms she would not we should miss,
She would possess the soul with fond regret,
She wills that here below we mourn her yet.

So, when declining Autumn comes apace,
She dons a robe that gold and purple grace,
With triple chaplet twined around her head,
Whose sparkling rays becoming lustre shed.

A garb of glistening topaz Nature wears,
With countless brilliants gemm'd—pure as her tears—
While from her white and sad despoilèd hands
One sees detached and falling floral bands.

Alors, à l'horizon devenu grave et sombre,
S'élève tout à coup la voix de l'aquilon,
Il sort en bondissant des abîmes de l'ombre,
Dissimulant la mort sur son noir tourbillon.

Il s'approche rapide, et la Nature tremble
Car elle connait trop ce hurlement lointain
Il sait que l'eunemi contre elle se rassemble
Que le trépas est près, et qu'il est son destin.

Et durant une nuit, quand le monde, tranquille,
Repose doucement en un calme sommeil,
Dans son tombeau béant elle glisse immobile . . .
Et l'hiver nous salue à l'heure de réveil.

Then in th' horizon, gloomy now and weird,
The north wind's voice is, on a sudden, heard:
Forth is he speeding from the depths of shade
Semblance of death his dark'ning storm has made.

He comes full swiftly, Nature quakes with fear,
Too well she knows the distant roar. And near
She sees the hostile forces congregate,
The end is nigh, and her impending fate.

During one night, the world now hush'd to sleep,
Reposing calmly in its visions deep—
To her wide tomb her noiseless path will take,
. . . And Winter greets us when at morn we wake.

*No. IV.

Christmas Carol.

NOËL BOURGUIGNON.

J'ENTENDS par notre rue
   Passer les ménétriers,
  Ecoutez comme ils jouent
   Sur leurs hautbois des noëls :
    Nous devant le feu
    Pour le mieux
  Chantons en jusqu'à menuet.

En Décembre on vous sonne
  Des noëls tous les jours,
Des chantres la parole
  Le deplore aux carrefours.
   Nous devant, &c.

Les pauvres lavandières,
  Au son de leurs battoirs,
Chantent à la rivière
  Tête au vent les pieds mouillés,
   Nous devant, &c.

* Harmonised by A. H. Brown.

* No. IV.

Christmas Carol.

HEAR along the street
  The rural minstrels' strain,
Hark! how their songs they raise,
  Their Christmas-tide refrain—
    We, too, with zest before the fire
    Will carols sing and never tire.

In drear December days
  The waits their music bring,
While songsters as they pass
  Their wayside ditties sing,
    We too, &c.

The poor their work beguile,
  To joyous strains keep time—
'Mid wet and cold, the while
  They chant their humble rhyme.
    We, too, &c.

---

* Words adapted from the old French. Set to an ancient Bourguignon Melody (1701).

*No. V.
Ancient Christmas Carol.

FROM A FLEMISH COLLECTION ENTITLED "LA PHILOMÈLE SÉRAPHIQUE (*Tournay*, A.D. 1640).

CHANT DE NOËL.

Les Pasteurs—

'OÙ vient cette troupe d'anges,
Et tous les cieux pleins d'éclairs ?
Eh ! D'où viennent ces louanges
Qui résonnent dedans l'air ?

L'Ange—
Je vous chante une merveille,
Qui remplit tout ce bas lieu
D'une joie non pareille
De la part de ce grand DIEU.

Les Pasteurs—
Ange des cieux quelle est-elle ?
Déjà nous sentons l'ardeur
D'une divine étincelle,
Qui nous enflamme le cœur.

L'Ange—
C'est que le SAUVEUR du monde
Est né sur le point du jour,
Pour sauver toute âme immonde
Par un grand excès d'amour.

Les Bergers—
Dites-nous en quelle place—
Mais en quel palais d'honneur ?
Quelle ville et quelle race
A reçu tant de bonheur ?

---

* Published, with music, in "Church Bells."

No. V.

TRANSLATED FROM THE FRENCH, AND ADAPTED TO THE OLD MELODY.

CHRISTMAS CAROL.

The Shepherds—

WHENCE this Angel-host resplendent,
And the skies aglow with light?
Whence this minstrelsy transcendent,
Ecstasy of sound and sight?

The Angel—

Unto you I sing a wonder,
Filling all this earth below
With a joy that knows no equal,
E'en of those GOD can bestow.

The Shepherds—

What may this be, Heavenly Angel?
Thou already dost impart
Hope celestial, enkindling
Ardour that inflames our heart.

The Angel—

For mankind is found a SAVIOUR
Born, full soon, at break of day,
Souls to save by sin polluted—
Such His boundless love's display!

The Shepherds—

Nay, but tell us where to find Him,
In what halls of regal state?
What the city—what the people—
Whom such joy and bliss await?

L'Ange—
En Bethléem dans une étable
Vous trouverez cet enfant,
Q'un âne va charitable *
De son haleine échauffant.

Les Bergers—
En un temps si misérable?
Dedans un lieu si vilain!
Le palais plus honorable
Est dû au Dieu Souverain.

L'Ange—
Quittez votre bergerie,
Allez voir ce Roi nouveau
Près de sa mère Marie
Couvert d'un simple drapeau.

Les Bergers—
Qu' offrirons-nous pour hommage?
Je lui donnerai du lait,
De la crême, et du fromage—
Moi—un petit agnelet.
Portons-lui, donc, à l'envie,
Courons, courons promptement
Lui présenter notre vie
Et lui prêter le serment.

Chantons une chansonnette
Alentour de Son berceau :
Je jouerai de ma musette,
Et moi—de mon chalumeau †
Donc, commençons tous à dire
D'une dévote ferveur
Lira, liron, liran, lire,
Vive le petit Sauveur !

---

* Literally, "whom a kindly ass keeps warming with its breath."
† Latin "calamus"—a reed.

The Angel—
Lo! at Bethlehem a manger,
Where this Child is to be found!
Whom a kindly ass doth cherish
With its sympathy profound.

The Shepherds—
At a time so unpropitious?
And within so mean a place!
Scarcely earth's most noble palace
Could suffice our GOD to grace.

The Angel—
Shepherds, up, and quit your sheepfold,
Haste to see this new-born King,
Lying near His mother Mary,
Clad with simple covering.

The Shepherds—
What in homage shall we offer?
Let us give our humble store,
I—some milk, and I—a lambkin—
Gifts like these become the poor.
Let us not delay, but hasten,
With all speed our duty pay,
Life and all in deep devotion
We before Him now will lay.

Let us sing around His cradle
Welcome songs of lullaby,
I—with pipe, and I—with reed-flute,
Each with other we will vie.
In the fervour of devotion
We will laud and bless His Name,
Who to be our gracious SAVIOUR,
To this world in mercy came.

ADDENDA.

Acrostics.

No. I.

Double Acrostic on the Title on the Cross.

(HEXAMETERS.)

"And Pilate wrote a title and put it on the Cross, and there was written in . . . Latin—
'IESUS NAZARENUS REX IUDÆORUM.'"

I ESUS—summa manet semper TIBI gloria VERB I
*N AZΩPAIOΣ — adoratum et venerabile NOME N
R EX "facilè es Princeps" regum plorate MAGISTE R
†I udæorum insigne Decus, LUX TU quoque MUND I

I ESU Whom while on earth men so often saluted as RABB I
‡N AZARA! Name for aye of rever'd and adorable mentio N
R ULER now Supreme, once so lamented a MASTE R
†I srael's Glory art Thou, and the light of the world O RABBON I

---

* " Ναζωραῖος κληθήσεται."—*S. Matt.* ii. 23.

† S. Luke ii. 32. ‡ The Latin Name of Nazareth.

No. II.

On one of the Noblest Names of the Century.

A n agèd hero men have borne to rest,*
R eposing fitly 'neath the stately dome—
T hat spot where England's bravest and her best
H ave found, and still shall find a hallow'd home.
U nfolded in the years to come the scroll of fame,
R eveal'd shall be the deeds that gild thy honour'd Name.

D uty thy watch-word—at thy country's call,
U ndaunted thou by danger or by toil!
K indling the soldier's zeal, inspiring all
E ngag'd with thee, Britannia's foes to foil.

O n all thine exploits patriots love to dwell,
F adeless the laurels thou hast earn'd so well!

W hat Name, like thine, 'mid annals of the past
E ncircled with such deathless fame shall last,
L osing no lustre from the lapse of years,
L eft as the Nation's Heir-loom, still appears?
I ndia thy tale of prowess shall retain,
N or Portugal forget, nor grateful Spain,
G lory for England won, and peace for them,
T hou didst the desolating torrent stem
O f war's advance, and like a Leader tried and true,
N apoleon, all Europe's scourge, didst crush at WATERLOO.

---

* Born May 1st, A.D. 1769. Fell asleep Sept. 14th, A.D. 1852.

No. III.

In Memoriam.

N o pangs so keen were his whose lose we mourn,
A s oft since then one fondest heart have torn;
P ierc'd by the cruel darts he sank to sleep *
O n Afric's soil 'mid wide-spread sorrow deep.
L eft to our charge—the risk alas! too great—
E xpos'd to wily foeman's vengeful hate.
O what the mother's loss of one she lov'd so well
N o heart but hers can ever know—*Priez pour elle.*

E ndear'd to all he met, that soldier youth
U ntaught in pride, of noble faith and truth,
G oes forth in England's cause renown to win,
†" E mérite" now—ere fame in arms begin.
N ay France, we claim thy Son—*Il n'est pas tout à vous—*
E ngland laments her warrior young—*Il est à nous.*

L ong shall we grieve for thee—long hold thee in renown
O Scion of Imperial House with thee cast down!
U nmindful of the past e'en foes thy lot must rue
I n grief profound.—And as that early grave they view
S *es amis à ce fils et pour sa mère disent leur A-dieu.*

---

* The French Prince Imperial was killed in South Africa while serving with British Troops.

† " Se dit d'un fonctionnaire en retraite
Jouissant des honneurs de son titre."
Latin-*Emeritus.*   —*P. Larousse.*

No. IV.

In Memoriam.

"*Vir et consilii magni et virtutis.*"—CÆSAR.

G ens longè latèque dolet, clarissime Miles,
O ptime te Civis, luget miransque Senatus :
R aro Ductorem aspiciet grata Anglia talem.
D ira tui nobis leti vix certa susurra !
" O si falsa forent ! " clamabat vox iterata.
N unquam evanescet posthac tua fama perennis.

G rief for her Son the Nation feels—for worth so peerless,
O 'er him a grateful Senate mourns its Chieftain fearless.
R are noble souls like his ! of lofty moral beauty,
*D ead to all love of self, forsaking all for duty !
O n names so great there rests a halo bright with glory,
N e'er may Posterity forget his wondrous story.

March 5th, A.D. 1885.

---

* " N'avait-il pas atteint cette abnégation de soi-même où quelques anachorètes sont parvenus ? Ce sacrifice complet de toutes les affections humaines, ne fut-il pas en lui presque accompli ? "—*Xavier de Maistre.*

No. V.
In Memoriam.

B ravely from early youth to manhood's prime
E ach rugged path the future statesman trod,
N o recreant spirit his—fame's steep to climb
J udicious steps he took—his feet with patience shod.
A learnèd Son he was of learnèd Sire,
M aturing by Life's wayside lofty aim;
I mpell'd by in-born worth he must aspire,
N e'er daunted by the sense of frequent failure's shame. ‡

D imly the dream of future greatness rose,
I nciting him to toil with ceaseless care :
S lowly but surely fond ambition grows,
R evealing wealth of mental powers of value rare.
A lert to note how "*Manners makyth man*" *
E nrolling characters for fiction's page,
L ordly or lowly features apt to scan,
I nscribing deftly traits of youth or riper age.

L eader of men shall their Portrayer be!
O bserv'd full soon by Rulers in the State. †
R oom for the "coming man!" Say "Who is he?"—
‡ D efeat at first, anon shall triumph him await !

---

* Ancient motto of Winchester, where he was at school, and New College, Oxford.

† After a contest with Earl Grey's son (Premier then of England) he, Earl Grey, enquired concerning Disraeli, "Who is he?"

‡ Unsuccessful at Chipping Wycombe, Marylebone, and Taunton.

ACROSTICS.

*B affled when erst his mark he fain would make,
E ssaying in the Senate foes to meet :—
A round "Young England" gather'd, him they take
C onscious of one with leading qualities replete.
O nward his course 'gainst adverse wind and tide,
N one else as he could weather stormy blast,
S afely the bark 'mid troubled seas to guide,
F irmly he nail'd his country's colours to the mast.
I mpregnable her realm if sons, like him, be true!
E ngland must ever faithful be to "Church and Queen,"
L et "Peace with honour" now prevail with her anew;
D evoted hearts shall keep for aye his memory green.

April 14*th*, A.D. 1885.

---

* On making his maiden speech in the House of Commons against his opponent O'Connell, the House would not hear him, "I am not at all surprised," were his closing words, "I have begun several times many things and I have often succeeded at last. I sit down now, but the time will come when you will listen to me."

No. VI.

In Memoriam.

A Humble Tribute to a Great Name.

"After he had served his own generation by the will of God, fell on sleep."

E ndear'd to English hearts that learn'd to prize
A soul of true Nobility like thine,
R ever'd thy blameless life! Thy counsels wise
L eave impress on this age, and still shall shine.

I n thee a grateful Nation mourns a Son
D evoid of guile, so gentle, tried, and true,
D evoted to her welfare:—thou hast won
E ncomium so just, earn'd by so few!
S incerely England's Senate grieves for thee,
L osing a trusty Leader in the State; *
E nduring honours from Posterity
I n fond remembrance shall thy Name await.
G reat Name! † abroad well known, at home so dear;
H onour'd alike by Queen, by People, and by Peer.

January 13th, A.D. 1887.

---

* "He is a man of scrupulous honour, of upright, blameless life; a man who has unshrinkingly given himself at all times to the service of the highest cause which he knew—the cause of the welfare of his fellow-man."—*Spoken by the* Solicitor-General, *the night before Lord Iddesleigh fell asleep so suddenly.*

† "He that is slow to anger is better than the mighty; and he that ruleth his spirit than he that taketh a city."—*Prov. xvi.* 32.

No. VII.
In Memoriam.

"When the ear heard me, then it blessed me." *

W eep, fair Devonia, for thy noble son,
I n full ripe honour'd age his race is run,
L ife, liv'd like his, a deathless record leaves:
L ordly his ancestry, yet worth achieves
I ts greater glory in the roll of fame,
A nd dignifies an else exalted name.
M ore lustrous when unsullied by the breath of shame.

R ever'd alike by peasant as by peer,
E nrich'd by * blessings to the Christian dear,
G ain'd by his gentle deeds from lowly hearts,
I nspired by Love which aye true charm imparts.
"N OBLESSE OBLIGE"—the motto of his life.
A partisan—yet foe to party strife,
L iving for others:—duty, nobly done,
D eserves each grateful tribute he so justly won. ‡

E ncourag'd by that life, men learn to brave
A "sea of troubles"; for above the wave
R ises the shining gleam, whose kindly light †
L eft to posterity remains a beacon bright!

D EVONIA wills her famous sons to grace:
E nduring monuments ‡ she fain would place,
V aunting how two twin natures foremost stood
O f all her scions, earning for her race
 N o fairer title than THE GENTLE AND THE GOOD.

November 20th, A.D. 1888.

---

† "Quod verum tutum"—Legend of the family escutcheon.
‡ The two statues of—Earl Iddesleigh, on Northernhay, and Earl Devon, in Bedford Circus, Exeter. That of Earl Devon was erected during his lifetime.

No. VIII.
In Memoriam.

J ames Abram Garfield—Name henceforth enshrined
A mid the records of Earth's Good and Great!
M ourn we in him a loss to human kind.
E ngland throughout her realm from each Estate
S alutes in sympathetic tones her Sister State.

A like from hall and cot from *Mart and Throne
B lends the sad unison of grief sincere,
R ecording how true greatness Nations own,
A nd hold, in common, noble Natures dear,
M ade thus akin, however far or near.

G reat are the lessons of his chequer'd life—
A purpose firm, with ever lofty aim,
R evering truth, stern foe to party strife,
F riend of the poor, who aye his help could claim †
I n him " 'twixt words and ways the just accord " ‡
E ndear'd to countless hearts—their loss his gain—
L ong his career true teaching shall afford,
D eprived of life too soon—yet lived he not in vain.

Sept. 27*th,* A.D. 1881.

---

* The Royal Exchange, London, was closed on the afternoon of his funeral.

† "An old gardener said to his mistress, 'O, ma'am, we felt somehow or other as if he belonged to us.'"—*Speech of Hon. J. Russell Lowell at a meeting of American citizens.*

‡ " J'admirai son héroïque simplicité, *l'heureux accord de ses paroles et de ses manières,* du son de la voix avec les expressions ; tout en lui me révélait un homme supérieur."—*Rouget de l'Isle, on Lazare Hoche.*

No. IX.

In Memoriam.

"One touch of Nature makes the whole world kin."

J OIN, Albion, to share Columbia's grief,
A s downcast in her loss she "sits alone,"
M ourning for one among her sons in chief.
E ngland, lamenting, fails not him to own
S on of adoption, well-belov'd, and widely known.*

R are gifts united mark'd a well-spent life;
U nsullied by the widespread taint of ill;
S triving in virtue's cause—the noblest strife,
S trong in her strength his duty to fulfil;
E ndued with meekness, yet with iron will.
L eading the van 'gainst foes of freedom's cause,
L eaving his lasting mark; his no short-lived applause.

L ove for the older country in him grew,†
O ppression's enemy on every hand;
W elding the bonds of brotherhood anew, ‡
E nhancing friendship for his native land.
L ong shall his words and deeds be known to fame,
L ong shall Britannia's sons revere his name.

August 15th, A.D. 1891.

---

* "We look upon him, indeed, as nearly English as ourselves."

† "The pleasant thing is to find one of the foremost of American poets and essayists . . . finding it impossible to look upon an Englishman as other than a racial brother."

‡ "He was our generous appreciator, but he always felt that the appreciation was family feeling."—"*Western Morning News*" Leader, *August 15th.*

W

No. X.

In Memoriam.

E ngland and England's Church have lost in thee,
D ear Primate, one whose kindly sympathy,
W orld-wide, and felt on many a distant strand,
A rous'd for Zion of their Fatherland
R enewal of men's love. . . . Yet when thy brothers come,
D estin'd to find thy spirit fled from Lambeth's home.*

W orthy thou wast to fill Augustin's chair.
H is missionary spirit thou didst share,
I n thine intent it was to celebrate
T he Primacy's remote yet memorable date †
E nrich'd in after times with names so good and great.

B elov'd so widely thou ! Thy courtesy
E ndear'd the lowly and the great to thee.
N o helmsman could the ark of CHRIST's Church steer
S o bravely well in times of doubt and fear.
O sainted soul, who didst of future glory sing, ‡
N ow hast thou reach'd at last the Palace of thy King.

---

* The Lambeth Conference, to which over 200 Bishops were invited for next year.

† A.D. 596.

"He was devoted to the services of the Church of England, and his mind was full to the last, as his letters show, of two events—one the celebration in this Cathedral of the thirteen-hundredth anniversary of the introduction of Christianity to Southern England; the other the great meeting of the Bishops at the Lambeth Conference."—*Dean Farrar, preaching in Canterbury Cathedral, on Sunday, October 11th, the day of the Archbishop's decease.*

From a Hymn by the Archbishop (H. A. & M., 505).

"For there to give the second birth
In mysteries and signs,
The Face of CHRIST o'er all the earth
On kneeling myriads shines,
‡ And if so fair, beyond compare,
Thine earthly Houses be,
In how great grace shall we Thy Face
In Thine own Palace see?"

Oct. 13*th*, A.D. 1896.

"WHAT ARE THESE FACES?
MEN OF ESTIMATION AND COMMAND."
Shakespeare.

www.ingramcontent.com/pod-product-compliance
Lightning Source LLC
Chambersburg PA
CBHW030008240426
43672CB00007B/867